GALORE PARK

So you really want to learn

Junior English

Book 1

Andrew Hammond MA

Series Editor: Susan Elkin MA BA (Hons) Cert Ed

www.galorepark.co.uk

Published by Galore Park Publishing Ltd
19/21 Sayers Lane, Tenterden, Kent TN30 6BW
www.galorepark.co.uk

Design by Design Gallery
Typsetting by Typetechnique
Illustrations by Rosie Brooks, Ian Douglass and Simon Tegg; cover illustration Gwyn Williamson

Printed by Replika Press, India

ISBN-13: 978 1 902984 82 7

First published 2007, reprinted 2008, 2010, 2011
An answer book is available to accompany this book:
ISBN-13: 978 1 902984 87 2

Details of other Galore Park publications are available at www.galorepark.co.uk

ISEB Revision Guides, publications and examination papers may also be obtained from Galore Park.

The publishers are grateful for permission to use the extracts and photographs as follows:

Extract from Animal Friends by Dick King-Smith reproduced with permission of AP Watt Ltd on behalf of Fox Busters Ltd; extract from First Encyclopedia of Animals Copyright © Kingfisher Publications Plc. Reproduced by permission of the publisher, all rights reserved; extract from Three Indian Princesses by Jamila Gavin published by Egmont, reproduced with permission; extract from The Changing Face of: India by David Cumming, edited by Alison Cooper. Reproduced by permission of Hodder and Stoughton Limited; extract from The Witches by Roald Dahl published by Jonathan Cape Ltd & Penguin Books, reproduced with permission; extract from The Secret World of Magic by Rosalind Kerven, with illustrations by Wayne Anderson, published by Frances Lincoln Ltd., © 2006. Reproduced with permission of Frances Lincoln Ltd., 4 Torriano Mews, Torriano Avenue, London NW5 2RZ; extract from Robert Louis Stevenson's Treasure Island, retold by Angela Wilkes. Reproduced from Treasure Island by permission of Usborne Publishing, 83–85 Saffron Hill, London EC1N 8RT, UK. www.usborne.com Copyright © 1982 Usborne Publishing Ltd; extract from Maps and Mapping Copyright © Kingfisher Publications Plc. Reproduced by permission of the publisher, all rights reserved; extract from History Diaries: The Diary of a Young Roman Girl by Moira Butterfield, first published in the UK by Franklin Watts, a division of The Watts Publishing Group Ltd, 338 Euston Road, London NW1 3BH; Good Company by Leonard Clark, in Classic Poems to Read Aloud selected by James Berry reproduced with permission of the Literary Executor of Leonard Clark; extract from e.explore: Insect by David Burnie (Dorling Kindersley, 2005). Text Copyright © 2005 Dorling Kindersley Limited; extract from Roald Dahl's Charlie and the Chocolate Factory – A Play, adapted by Richard George published by Penguin Books, reproduced with permission; chocolate fudge cake recipe courtesy of www.sainsburys.co.uk; extract from Dog Days by Geraldine McCaughrean. Reproduced by permission of Hodder and Stoughton Limited; extract from The History News: In Space written by Michael Johnstone. Text © 1999 Michael Johnstone. Reproduced by permission of Walker Books Ltd, London SE11 5HJ; extract from The Butterfly Lion by Michael Morpurgo reprinted by permission of HarperCollins Publishers Ltd. © Michael Morpurgo 1996; extract from Max Fax: Big Cats by Claire Llewellyn. Reproduced by permission of Hodder and Stoughton Limited.

Photo credits: P17 Getty Images, P90 Robert Stainforth/ Alamy, P101 NASA/Science Photo Library, P113 Gregory Dimijian/Science Photo Library

Acknowledgements

My thanks go to the students, staff and parents around me who have, in their own ways, helped me in preparing this first volume in the *Junior English* series.

Thanks also to Susan Elkin and Nick Oulton for their continued editorial support. It is a pleasure to work for such similar pedants for punctuation and sticklers for style.

Finally my thanks to Andrea, Henry, Nell and young Edward for their continued patience while Daddy writes his books.

A.J.H.

Preface

This is the first volume in the three-part series of *Junior English*, which, I hope, serves as a fitting prequel to the much acclaimed *So you really want to learn English* series by Susan Elkin.

In choosing the texts, writing the questions and preparing the wide range of related tasks that follow each excerpt, I have tried, at all times, to offer readers an enjoyable and stimulating mix of old and new, whilst maintaining the quality and rigour you would expect from a prep school resource. The National Curriculum, the National Literacy Strategy and the new Core Learning Skills of the Primary Framework all play their part in this collection, but they do not eclipse the stalwarts of good education, namely creativity and some good old-fashioned common sense.

I hope that through this, and the other titles in the series, the teaching and learning of English in your classroom continues to be a hugely beneficial and fun experience for pupil and pedant.

A.J.H.

Contents

Chapter 4

Chapter 5

Chapter 6

Chapter 7

Introduction

Hidden deep between the covers of this little book, there lies some of the most important advice you will ever find: how to make a treasure map; how to biff a badger on the bottom; how to turn children into mice; and, most importantly of all, how to make chocolate fudge cake.

It is amazing what you can find in a little book. You will encounter some astonishing animals too. From Goliath beetles to tiny fleas, not to mention the odd disgruntled badger. You will even meet the famous whale who came to London.

All this and you don't even have to leave your classroom! Such is the beauty of reading. It is an important skill for us all to learn — probably the most important skill there is. For reading helps us to learn: learn how to speak, how to write, perhaps even how to think.

Just think about it. Imagine what you would know if you had never read any books at all. Not much. Only what you had seen or heard, probably. There is the television, of course, and some programmes can teach you quite a bit. But there is one thing that television can't do. It can't develop your imagination. And just as reading is the most important skill you possess, your imagination is the most precious tool you have. Only through reading, and thinking, and scrunching your face up tight until you look like a shrivelled apricot, will you stretch your imagination.

So, in some ways, this book is a guide to doing just that — to reading, and thinking, and stretching your imagination. But it is something else: it is a collection of interesting lessons in how to improve the way you communicate to others, through speaking and writing. During the course of this book, you will have lots of opportunities to talk to one another: to join in class discussions and debates, to perform role-plays with your friends, and to deliver class talks and presentations. You will find yourself writing a great deal too: from wizards' diaries to treasure maps, from short stories of pirates and princesses to spidery poems, not to mention your own recipe book for magic potions.

Talking and writing, listening and reading can be lots of fun. But they can be difficult things to do. Sometimes you may feel you just want to give up and say, 'Reading's not for me, thank you very much' or 'I don't think I'll join in today,

I've got nothing to say'. We all have these kinds of days, but the good news is they never last. They are usually followed by sunnier days, when you feel like joining in, chatting until you burst and scribbling until your hand hurts.

So read this little book and try to join in all the interesting activities it brings, remembering all the time that you are practising some very important skills along the way.

Enjoy that chocolate fudge cake. And stay away from badgers.

A.J.H.

Chapter 1

Badger biffing

Never upset a badger. As Dick King-Smith knows, they can be full of surprises…

I bet there aren't many people who can say, 'Once I biffed a badger on the bottom with my hat.'

I can. I was going out early one summer's morning to fetch the cows in for milking. On my way I had to cross a big pasture, and there, right in the

5   middle of it, was a badger.

Now, badgers are nocturnal animals and, though there was a big sett in the nearby wood where we often heard them clucking and chattering at night, it wasn't often that we saw them in broad daylight.

So I hurried towards this solitary badger, hoping that it wouldn't run away

10 till I'd had a good look at it. It didn't run away. It didn't take the slightest notice of me, even though I was now standing right beside it. It just carried on snuffling about in the grass.

I felt rather foolish. I took off my hat and biffed the badger gently on its bottom.

15 It didn't even look up. 'What's up with you, my friend?' I said. 'You deaf, or blind, or both?'

Slowly, with that rolling bear-like shuffle that badgers have, it began to move towards the wood, while I continued to beat a light tattoo on its backside. Until, at last, it came to a hole in the hedge, and disappeared.

20 The very next morning I went exactly the same way to fetch the dairy herd, and there, in exactly the same place, were two badgers. My friend, I thought, and his friend!

Happily I ran towards them. With a volley of furious grunts, the two badgers charged at me. I fled at top speed.

25 Nobody ever believes this story.

But it's true.

(From Animal Friends by Dick King-Smith, 1996)

Exercise 1.1

Read the passage from *Animal Friends*. Then answer these questions in proper sentences.

1. What was the author on his way to do when he saw the badger?

2. Where was the badger?

3. (a) How did the badger react to the author?

   (b) Do you think it was frightened by this visitor?

4. Why did the author think the badger might be 'deaf or blind, or both'?

5. How was the badger's reaction different when the author saw him, and his friend, the next day?

6. Why do you think the badger had returned to the same spot, this time with a friend?

7. Use a dictionary to find out what these words mean: (a) *biffed* (line 1); (b) *nocturnal* (line 6); (c) *sett* (line 6); (d) *solitary* (line 9).

Garden friends

How well do you know the animals in your garden? Here are some fascinating facts about a few of them.

Badger   Badgers are powerful creatures, but they are also shy. They are related to skunks and, like them, have black and white markings. In Europe, they live in family groups in woodlands. Badgers are most active in the evening. This is when they come out to feed and to collect straw for bedding.

Bat   Bats have big ears, furry bodies and wings like leather. They are nocturnal mammals. This means they sleep in caves and attics during the day and fly out to feed at night-time.

Hedgehog   Hedgehogs are mammals found in the woods and hedges of Europe, Asia and Africa. Most have thousands of thick spines covering their backs, which help to protect them from predators. There are also hairy hedgehogs, which live in Asia.

Mole   Moles are small mammals that spend almost all their lives underground. We know they are around because of the molehills they create when digging their tunnels. They live in Europe, Asia and North America. Big powerful front paws, a pointed nose and sharp claws mean that moles are excellent diggers.

20 **Owl**   Owls are birds of prey that hunt mainly at night. They use their sensitive hearing and large eyes (which give them good night vision) to catch animals such as mice and rabbits. Owls have soft feathers that allow them to fly silently. The hooting cry of some species is easy to recognise.

25 **Squirrel**   Most squirrels have big, bushy tails and live in trees. They are active during the day, running from branch to branch in search of nuts, fruit and seeds. Squirrels love seeds like acorns, which they gnaw with their sharp front teeth. In autumn, they sometimes bury a supply in the ground to last

30   them through the winter.

(From First Encyclopedia of Animals, Kingfisher, 1998)

Exercise 1.2

Read the passage entitled *Garden friends*. Then answer these questions in proper sentences.

1. In what way are badgers similar to skunks?

2. Where are you most likely to find a bat during the daytime?

3. How do hedgehogs protect themselves from predators?

4. How would you know if there were moles in your garden?

5. Why are owls particularly good at catching mice and rabbits, even at night?

6. How are squirrels able to feed during the cold winter months?

7. If you could be any of the six animals in the extract, which would you be, and why?

8. Use a dictionary to find meanings for the following words: (a) *shy* (line 1); (b) *mammals* (line 7); (c) *predators* (line 12); (d) *gnaw* (line 28).

Exercise 1.3 ✏️

Your turn to write:

1. Read the passage about badger biffing again. Imagine you are the first badger in the story. What do you think of this visitor? How do you like being biffed on the bottom? Rewrite some of the story from the badger's point of view. Write in the first person (I/me), as if the badger is speaking.

2. Have you ever had a strange meeting with an animal, like the one in *Badger biffing*? Have you ever spotted a rare animal in an unlikely place? Write about a time when you have been surprised by an animal, either in your garden or in the wild.

3. Write a story about the nocturnal animals in your garden. Every night they wait until you are safely tucked up in bed and then meet to share stories and get up to mischief! What will they do tonight...?

4. Suppose you are helping to create an encyclopaedia of animals. Write some sentences about the following animals: *cow, sheep, pig, chicken, goat, horse*. Remember to present them in alphabetical order.

. . . .

Learning about language

Nouns (naming words)

A noun is a naming word which shows us the name of a person, place or thing. For example:

Rosie   France   pencil

Just as the world around us is full of people, places and things, so our language is full of nouns.

Look at the following sentence from the first passage. It contains four nouns.

*I took off my **hat** and biffed the **badger** gently on its **bottom**.*

Exercise 1.4

Look carefully at these sentences. Write them out. Then underline the noun(s). Remember: you are looking for people, places or things. Sometimes the noun is plural – more than one. For example: **books**, **teachers**, **forests**.

1. The author met a badger in a field.

2. The badger returned the next day with a friend.

3. Bats have big ears, furry bodies and wings like leather.

4. They sleep in caves and attics during the day.

5. Hedgehogs have thick spines covering their backs.

6. Most squirrels have big, bushy tails and live in trees.

Collective nouns

Collective nouns tell us the name of a group of animals, such as a **flock** of sheep, a **herd** of pigs or a **swarm** of bees.

Although a collective noun names a group of animals, it is treated as a single unit: **a** pride of lions, or **a** peep of chickens.

Exercise 1.5

Write a sentence for each of these phrases. Then underline the collective noun in each sentence. Look at the example:

*a pride of lions – I saw a **pride** of lions in the safari park.*

1. a clutch of chicks

2. a labour of moles

3. a shoal of fish

4. a squabble of seagulls

5. a warren of rabbits

6. a parade of elephants

Capital letters

Every sentence begins with a capital letter, as this one did.

Capital letters are sometimes called 'Upper Case' or 'Caps'. Capital letters are also used to begin the names of people and places. For example:

Mary and Joe travelled to London.

Capital letters are often used for titles and headings, too:

Harry Potter and the Philosopher's Stone

Fire Safety Instructions

In stories, sometimes an author may wish to emphasise one or more words, and so will use capital letters to make the words STAND OUT. This is often used in story speech:

'I DON'T WANT TO GO!' yelled Daniel.

'I am NOT listening!' said his mother.

'I'm REALLY sorry,' he said.

Exercise 1.6

Rewrite these sentences, putting capital letters where you think they should be.

1. on the way home, david and his family stopped for lunch.

2. when lucy arrived in bristol, she went shopping.

3. 'the train to portsmouth is leaving in three minutes,' said the guard.

4. have you read any books by roald dahl?

5. 'we've been waiting for ages,' said mum. 'hurry up!'

6. 'will mrs jackson please come to reception,' said elizabeth.

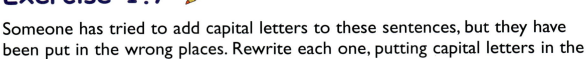

Exercise 1.7

Someone has tried to add capital letters to these sentences, but they have been put in the wrong places. Rewrite each one, putting capital letters in the **correct** places.

1. on friday We went Swimming.

2. 'would you like To visit spain this Year?' asked leslie.

3. the crowd Cheered as england Scored a try against scotland in The final minute.

4. jane's teacher welcomed mr and mrs smith into the Classroom.

5. queen elizabeth Lives in buckingham palace, In london.

6. 'in march,' said loren, 'I am Going to switzerland for a skiing Holiday.'

Can you spell?

-dge

The letters **–dge** are often found together in words.
For example:

*ba**dge**r*   *he**dge**hog*

Can you hear the 'd' sound just before the softer 'g' in these words? Say them aloud. Remember to include the 'd' when you are writing words that contain this letter pattern.

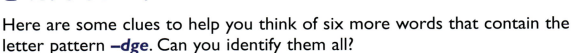

Exercise 1.8

Here are some clues to help you think of six more words that contain the letter pattern **–dge**. Can you identify them all?

1. A sweet, buttery treat, like chocolate.

2. A natural barrier separating two gardens.

3. To avoid a tackle.

4. To spread ink across the page.

5. A reward you can pin to your jumper.

6. Someone staying with you.

Exercise 1.9

Find the animals...

You may see the following animals in your garden. But can you spot them in a wordsearch?

Badger									
	e	t	n	d	l	z	a	t	o	h

Badger

Bat

Fox

Hedgehog

Mole

Mouse

Owl

Rabbit

Robin

Squirrel

e	t	n	d	l	z	a	t	o	h
l	y	x	w	r	w	m	e	u	e
o	q	b	o	n	f	o	x	k	d
m	y	b	b	e	z	u	t	j	g
i	i	m	a	r	t	s	i	q	e
n	o	j	t	d	b	e	b	t	h
o	h	v	u	i	g	v	b	q	o
l	q	z	d	h	a	e	a	s	g
w	d	e	s	d	t	c	r	n	z
l	e	r	r	i	u	q	s	o	c

Speaking and listening

1. Word tennis: in pairs, take turns to call out the name of a different animal. If one of you hesitates or repeats the name of an animal already said, then your partner wins a point. How long will your rally be before someone makes a mistake? You can vary the game by thinking of jungle animals, farm animals or garden animals only.

2. Find out about a particular garden animal – like a badger, squirrel or fox – and then give a class talk on it. Try to find out about its diet, where it sleeps, how long it may live for and where it comes from. Remember to use pictures as well as words, to keep your friends interested.

3. Play twenty questions: think of an animal and invite your friends to guess what it is. They may ask up to twenty questions, the answers to which may only be 'yes' or 'no'.

4. Put together a short role-play in pairs, in which you are two garden animals, chatting. The owner of the garden has been too busy to look after his garden, and you are quite disappointed to see it has become so overgrown. You just can't rely on these humans anymore! What would *you* do to make the garden better?

Have you read?

If you like animal adventures, you will certainly enjoy these stories:

The Railway Cat by Phyllis Arkle (Hodder Children's Books)
Hedgehogs Don't Eat Hamburgers by Vivian French & Chris Fisher (Puffin Books)
Dumpling by Dick King-Smith & Jo Davies (Puffin Books)
The Guard Dog by Dick King-Smith (Young Corgi)
The Sheep-Pig by Dick King-Smith (Puffin Books)
Fantastic Mr Fox by Roald Dahl (Puffin Books)
Beatrix Potter Complete Tales: The Complete Tales by Beatrix Potter (Frederick Warne)
The Dancing Bear by Michael Morpurgo (Collins)
The Butterfly Lion by Michael Morpurgo (Collins)
Charlotte's Web by E. B. White (Puffin Books)
Mrs Frisby and the Rats of Nimh by Robert C. O'Brien (Puffin Modern Classics)

PERFECT STORM
THE SNOWMAN

Other things to do...

- Keep a diary in which you list all the animals you see in your garden in one week. Note the name of each animal, with a short description, then record the time and the place that you saw it. Share your wildlife-watcher's diary in class. How many of you have similar animals visiting your gardens?

- Design a poster telling readers why it is good to have a pet at home. You could choose a dog or cat, or perhaps something unusual, like a snake or a pet tarantula. Use a mixture of pictures, diagrams and words on your poster.

- Write a poem all about your favourite animal by writing the name of the animal down the left-hand side of the poem, and use the letters to begin each line. This is called an **acrostic** poem. Then draw a colourful picture at the end.

Chapter 2

An Indian princess

Savitri was a beautiful princess who lived in India hundreds of years ago. Her eyes were like lotus flowers. Her skin was the colour of sunbeams. Her hair was shining and long and as black as night. Savitri was a very rich princess. Her sarees were made of the very finest silks, and she was
5 always covered in jewels.

Her home was a magnificent palace with large beautiful rooms to explore, and cool courtyards with fountains in which to rest. And all around were the palace gardens with their intricate flower beds, avenues of cypress trees, and shady paths among the guava groves. But over the
10 walls where the sun always set, where the rest of the world spread away to the shimmering horizon; over the wall was the jungle.

Savtiri could see the jungle from her balcony. She could hear the jungle from her bed. Each morning she loved to watch the green parrots burst upwards from the tree tops into the pink, dawn sky and swoop round
15 the palace. She loved to catch a glimpse of the spotted deer as they sprang through the dappled shadows; or the grey mongoose spinning and curling down the old, gnarled trunks of the trees. Sometimes she saw a small solemn boy herding dusty buffalo down to the river. Sometimes she saw the village children running almost naked through
20 the long grass only to disappear laughing and squealing into the jungle. How she longed to throw off her fine clothes and join them. How she longed to fling off her leather sandals and feel more than the hard, white marble beneath her feet.

One afternoon when her old ayah was dozing in the heat of day, the
25 gardener was bent intently over his rose bushes, and her chosen playmates were quarrelling on the swing, Savitri slipped away. From her balcony, she had often noticed a small door in the palace walls. Savitri was determined now to find this door. Hoisting up her saree, she ran through the palace gardens until she reached the high, grey boundary walls. Then
30 trailing her fingers along its ancient stones, she walked and walked for several minutes.

Suddenly, there it was. Just a small, wooden door. The only thing that stood between her and the outside world. She pushed and it opened. For a few moments Savitri stood absolutely still, just gazing in wonder.

35 There was the jungle not more than three paces away, green and dense and very, very wild.

saree or *sari*   a long garment worn by an Indian lady
ayah   a nursemaid in India

(From Three Indian Princesses, Jamila Gavin, 1987)

Exercise 2.1

Read the passage from *An Indian princess*. Then answer these questions in proper sentences.

1. In what ways could Savitri's eyes be 'like lotus flowers'? (line 2)?

2. How might you know that Savitri was rich, just by looking at her?

3. Name two animals that Savitri spotted in the jungle, beyond the palace walls.

4. Does Savitri want to enter the jungle? How do you know? Write one sentence that helps you to decide.

5. Explain in your own words how Savitri finally manages to enter the jungle.

6. Use a thesaurus to find an alternative word for each of the following adjectives: (a) *intricate* (line 8); (b) *shimmering* (line 11); (c) *solemn* (line 18); (d) *dense* (line 35).

Living in India

India is a colourful, exciting and historic country, full of different people and places. Find out what modern India means to Rati, Suraj, Bhupinder and Fay.

I'm Rati Fyzee and I was born in Bombay in 1922. It has recently had its name changed to Mumbai, but I will always call it Bombay. That's its proper name!

5 My city has changed beyond all recognition since the 1970s. So many high-rise buildings have sprung up, Bombay has become the Manhattan of India. The city is on a small peninsula, so we have had to build upwards rather than outwards on to neighbouring land.

All this building work has caused a lot of problems, particularly a leap in the population. The people who came here to build the new offices and flats
10 have stayed here, and now our slums are among the largest in the world.

*** *** ***

My name is Suraj. I'm 12 years old and I live in the capital city, New Delhi. We live in a block of flats with a hundred other families. During the summer it gets very hot and there are always power cuts, because everyone has their air-conditioners and fans working flat out. We have a
15 huge diesel generator that provides electricity when there is a power cut but the trouble is, it often breaks down. Then I miss my favourite TV serials. My mother says it's a good opportunity to do my homework – by candlelight!

At school we have been learning about alternative power such as solar
20 energy. We have so much sunshine in India that I think in future the government should use it to provide more electricity.

*** *** ***

My name is Bhupinder and I live with my parents, my grandmother and four brothers and sisters. You can see some of our neighbours in this photo too! In India there are too many people and not enough homes.
25 We are too poor to buy a house or flat, so we have to rent a room from my father's boss. It's 3 metres wide and 4 metres long – a tight fit for eight people, but we manage.

My mother cooks outside in the yard. There's also a hand-pump here for our water. Life is very hard for us. Every day I see how lucky other
30 families are and hope and pray that I can get a good job so that I can look after my parents when they are old.

***

I'm Fay Singh and I'm a graduate of Chundigarh University. After I received my degree in English I decided to travel around the world for a few months. When I came back to Delhi I found a job making travel
35 arrangements for business executives. Once it was assumed that women would stay at home and take care of the family. No more! Many women now have careers. Look at me: I'm only 30 years old, yet I'm in a high-powered job. I work hard and am respected for it.

(From The Changing Face of India, David Cumming, 2001)

Exercise 2.2 ✏

Read the passage entitled *Living in India* and then answer these questions in proper sentences.

1. Which of the four speakers in the passages is the oldest?

2. Why is building space on the ground so limited in Mumbai?

3. Why does Suraj experience so many power cuts during the summer in New Delhi?

4. According to Suraj, how could the government generate more electricity in the future?

5. Do you think Bhupinder has a tougher life than the other speakers? Give reasons to explain your answer.

6. (a) What does Fay Singh do for a living?

   (b) Why is she unusual, compared with the traditional image of Indian women?

Exercise 2.3 ✏

Your turn to write:

1. Imagine that Savitri's ayah (nursemaid) awakes to find her gone. What will she do? How will she find her? Continue this story in your own words, describing what might happen when Savitri is discovered missing.

2. Write a traditional story of your own about a prince or a princess who might have lived hundreds of years ago in a land far away. Include some magical fairy tale ingredients, like a palace, a dark forest, an evil enemy and a handsome hero.

3. Look again at the passage entitled *Living in India*. Read about the different people. Then put together a short paragraph which might be written next to a picture of <u>you</u> and <u>your</u> family. Think about: where you live; with whom you share your home; what you like to do in your spare time; any interesting facts about your town and country.

4. What do you know about India? Use atlases, encyclopaedias and websites. Then put together an information text on India. Include some interesting facts about its location, population, industries, food, customs, famous towns and places. Remember to include pictures, diagrams, maps, tables and lots of writing.

Learning about language

Adjectives (describing words)

An adjective, or describing word, often describes a nearby noun. Adjectives give us more information. They make sentences more interesting for the reader.

Look at these adjectives from *An Indian Princess*.

beautiful *princess*

magnificent *palace*

The adjective **beautiful** helps us to imagine how the princess looks, and the adjective **magnificent** makes us think of a very grand palace.

Adjectives usually come just before the noun that they are describing, but not always. Look at this sentence, which also describes the princess:

*Her hair was **shining** and **long**.*

The adjectives **shining** and **long** describe the noun 'hair', even though they come after it.

Exercise 2.4

Write down these sentences. Then underline the adjective(s) in each one.

1. The princess wore pretty sarees made of fine silk.

2. Savitri loved to watch the spotted deer as they sprang through the dappled shadows.

3. Sometimes she saw a small, solemn boy herding dusty buffalo down to the river.

4. The palace was surrounded by gardens with intricate flower beds and shady paths.

5. Savitri ran up to the high walls and ran her fingers across the ancient stones.

6. The jungle beyond the palace was green and dense.

Exercise 2.5

Each of these sentences contains a rather dull adjective. Replace each underlined adjective with a more interesting or accurate one. Use a thesaurus to help you.

1. Rati describes Mumbai as a <u>busy</u> city.

2. Suraj's home can become <u>hot</u> during the summer months.

3. They have a <u>big</u> generator to provide electricity when there is a power cut.

4. Life is <u>hard</u> for Bhupinder and his family.

5. Princess Savitri lived in a <u>nice</u> palace.

6. Savitri thought the jungle looked <u>good</u>.

Full stops

Full stops (.) show that a sentence has ended. Look at these examples, taken from the passages:

My mother cooks outside in the yard. There's also a hand-pump here for our water. Life is very hard for us.

Without full stops or capital letters, these sentences would be difficult to understand.

my mother cooks outside in the yard there's also a hand-pump here for our water life is very hard for us

Exercise 2.6

The following passage is taken from *An Indian Princess,* but all the capital letters and full stops have been removed, making it difficult to read. Rewrite the sentences, putting in capital letters and full stops wherever you think they are needed. (Look at the passage again for help.)

suddenly, there it was just a small, wooden door the only thing that stood between her and the outside world she pushed it and opened for a few moments savitri stood absolutely still, just gazing in wonder there was the jungle not more than three paces away, green and dense and very, very wild

Can you spell?

Adjective endings

In the story above, Princess Savitri was born in India. To show that she comes from India, we say she is Indian.

India becomes *Indian*

By adding **–n** to the name of the country, we can make an adjective, **Indian**. Similarly, a person who comes from America is Americ**an**. There are many countries that end in **–a** and these are easy to change:

Austria – Austrian

Africa – African

Jamaica – Jamaican

For some countries, however, you need to make more changes. For example:

Italy – Italian

Brazil – Brazilian

Some names of countries follow a different rule altogether when they become adjectives. If you are from England, for example, you are **English**; those who are born in France are *French* and people born in China are **Chinese**.

Exercise 2.7

Change the names of these countries into adjectives. You may need to use a dictionary to help you.

1. Malaysia
2. Australia
3. South Africa
4. Switzerland
5. Scotland

6. Hungary
7. Israel
8. Pakistan
9. Kenya
10. Ireland

Exercise 2.8

Write down the name of the country from which these adjectives have been made:

1. Spanish
2. Argentinian
3. Swedish
4. Dutch
5. Scottish

6. Chilean
7. Zimbabwean
8. Iranian
9. Norwegian
10. Welsh

Speaking and listening

1. Work with a partner. One of you is a person in the passage entitled *Living in India*. The other person can be him or herself. Find out more about one another – where you go to school, hobbies and interests, sports, etc. Perform these role-play conversations for the class.

2. Take turns to be Savitri, or another person in the second passage, and sit in the 'hot seat' at the front of the class. Then answer questions from your friends, in the role of that person. Try to imagine how he or she might answer each question.

3. Imagine that you are Princess Savitri. You have just returned to the palace after sneaking into the jungle for a while. Your nursemaid is waiting for you – and she looks very angry! Working with a friend, role-play a conversation between Savitri and her ayah.

4. Put together a short presentation – either on your own or with a friend – about a particular country that you find interesting. You may have been there, or it may be your dream to travel there one day. What do you like about this country? Share some information about this country, and explain why you would like to visit it.

Have you read?

Here are some enjoyable stories which involve exciting journeys and interesting tales from around the world:

Seasons of Splendour: Tales, Myths and Legends of India by Madhur Jaffrey & Michael Foreman (Puffin Books)
Kensuke's Kingdom by Michael Morpurgo (Egmont Books)
The Firework-maker's Daughter by Phillip Pullman (Corgi Yearling Books)
Grandpa's Indian Summer by Jamila Gavin (Egmont Books)
Grandpa Chatterji by Jamila Gavin (Egmont Books)
The Warrior and the Moon by Nick Would (Frances Lincoln Children's Books)
African Folk Tales by Hugh Vernon-Jackson (Dover Publications)

Other things to do...

- Give a short class talk about India. You might use the information text that you made on India for the writing task earlier in this chapter. Use pictures and sounds to help keep your presentation lively and interesting. You may be able to use Microsoft PowerPoint for your talk.

- Are you proud to be living where you do? What do you like about this country, and what would you like to change? Make notes. Then share your thoughts in a class discussion.

- What is your nationality? In which country were you born? Imagine that you are working as a tourism officer in your home country. Think about why foreign tourists should travel to your country for a holiday. What is so good about it? Write a short travel brochure, advertising fantastic holidays in your country.

Chapter 3

A witch's song

Have you ever met nastier witches than these? And what a strange way of talking they have…

"Down vith children! Do them in!
Boil their bones and fry their skin!
Bish them, sqvish them, bash them, mash them!
Brrreak them, shake them, slash them, smash them!
5 Offer chocs vith magic powder!
Say 'Eat up!' then say it louder.
Crrram them full of sticky eats,
Send them home still guzzling sveets.
And in the morning little fools
10 Go marching off to separate schools.
A girl feels sick and goes all pale.
She yells, 'Hey look! I've grrrown a tail!'
A boy who's standing next to her
Screams, 'Help! I think I'm growing fur!'
15 Another shouts, 'Vee look like frrreaks!
There's viskers growing on our cheeks!'
A boy who vos extremely tall
Cries out, 'Vot's wrong? I'm grrrowing small!'
Four tiny legs begin to sprrrout
20 From everybody rrround about.
And all at vunce, all in a trrrice,
There are no children! Only MICE!
In every school is mice galore
All rrrunning rrround the school-rrroom floor!
25 And all the poor demented teachers
Is yelling, 'Hey, who are these crrreatures?'
They stand upon the desks and shout,
'Get out, you filthy mice! Get out!
Vill someone fetch some mouse-trrraps, please!
30 And don't forrrget to bring the cheese!'
Now mouse-trrraps come and every trrrap

Goes *snippy-snip* and *snappy-snap*.
The mouse-trrraps have a powerful spring,
The springs go *crack* and *snap* and *ping*!
35 Is lovely noise for us to hear!
Is music to a vitch's ear!
Dead mice is every place arrround,
Piled two feet deep upon the grrround,
Vith teachers searching left and rrright,
40 But not a single child in sight!
The teachers cry, 'Vot's going on?
Oh vhere have all the children gone?
Is half-past nine and as a rrrule
They're never late as this for school!'
45 Poor teachers don't know vot to do.
Some sit and rrread, and just a few
Amuse themselves throughout the day
By sweeping all the mice avay.
AND ALL US VITCHES SHOUT HOORAY!"

(From The Witches by Roald Dahl, 1983)

Exercise 3.1 🖍

Read *A witch's song*. Then answer these questions in proper sentences.

1. What happened to the children before they all turned into mice?

2. Do the teachers like the mice? How can you tell?

3. There is a rhyming pattern in this poem. Describe it in your own words.

4. Why do you think the author uses words like 'vill' instead of *will* and 'brrreak' instead of *break*? What effect do these words have when you read the poem?

5. What do you think of the witches, now that you have read their song? What have you learned about them?

6. Use a dictionary to find the meanings of these words: (a) *guzzling* (line 8); (b) *galore* (line 23); (c) *demented* (line 25); (d) *amuse* (line 47).

A world of magic

How much do you think you know about the world of magic? Read on to find out about spells, wishing wells and dragons who live in crystal palaces…

Magic spells

Imagine performing impossible deeds! Imagine enchanting someone! Imagine changing something completely! Magic spells can do all this.

Four ways to cast a spell

5
- Chant secret words in a mysterious language.
- Collect spiders' webs, frog-spawn and other weird ingredients from forests and wild places, then brew them up in a steaming cauldron.
- Wear or wave a magic object – a cloak, cap, wand or staff.
- Touch the object of your spell or blow on it gently.

10 ### A spell can…
- Send someone into a long, deep sleep.
- Open a door in a solid rock.
- Carry someone across the world in a flash.
- Make people and things invisible.

15 Wishes

In fairy tales, wishes always used to come true.

- Old wise women sometimes granted wishes as a reward to kind children who had helped them.
- Fairies often gave three wishes to people they liked.
20 - You could wish on a star, or over a magic ring.

You could make a wish just by saying, 'I wish I had…' and whatever you wanted would appear by magic. Nowadays wishing takes longer – but it can still work!

Wishing wells

25 Castles, gardens and even shopping centres sometimes have a wishing well. If you see one, throw a coin into the water, close your eyes and make a wish!

Wish-bones

If your family has a roast chicken for dinner, ask for the wish-bone 30 afterwards. Get someone to help you pull it until it breaks in half. The person who gets the bigger part can make a wish.

Be careful how you wish!

- Keep your wish secret, or it won't come true.
- Make it clear exactly what you are wishing for.
35 - Don't wish for the wrong thing by mistake.
- Don't wish for something selfish – it will lead to trouble.
- Don't waste your wish – you won't get another one.

Secret worlds

Scientists think that there are many other worlds out in space. Some 40 people say there are magical worlds hidden here on Earth too.

Sky world

There is a secret world far above the skies of Africa and America. You can reach it by climbing a rope or a ladder hanging down from the clouds, or from a tree so tall that its highest branches are invisible. In the Sky 45 World, magic creatures live with the Sun, Moon and stars.

Fairyland

A magic world of fairies and dwarves lies deep below the ground. The countryside of England, Ireland, Scotland and Wales is dotted with caves and rock doors leading into it.

50 ### Dragon realms

At the seaside in China, Japan and Korea, the waves sometimes fall apart to reveal a golden path. It leads down to the underwater realm of the dragons! Here, fierce dragon kings and beautiful dragon princesses live in shimmering crystal palaces with silk furnishings. Their servants are
55 fish, lobsters and crabs.

The dragon kings don't get many human visitors. If you ever find your way down there, they will be very peased to see you. They might even give you a wonderful gift.

(From The Secret World of Magic by Rosalind Kerven, with illustrations by Wayne Anderson, 2006)

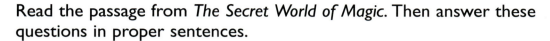

Exercise 3.2

Read the passage from *The Secret World of Magic*. Then answer these questions in proper sentences.

1. Name two ingredients you might place in a cauldron to make a magic spell.

2. What two things can a spell do?

3. (a) Where might you still see a wishing well today?

   (b) What should you do if you find one?

4. What is so special about a wish-bone?

5. How can you enter the Sky World?

6. Which parts of this passage do you believe? Write your own thoughts about spells, wishes and magic worlds.

7. Find dictionary definitions for the following words: (a) *enchanting* (line 2); (b) *cauldron* (line 7); (c) *realm* (line 52); (d) *furnishings* (line 54).

Exercise 3.3

Your turn to write:

1. Write your own rhyming poem about witches and wizards. Think about the kinds of spells they might cast, and the ingredients they need for their magic potions...

2. Have you ever been somewhere that you thought was haunted? An old castle perhaps, or a dark forest? Choose a real or imaginary place and describe it for the reader. Try to use lots of interesting description to bring the place to life (and frighten your reader!).

3. If you could have one special, magical power, what would it be, and why? Describe this power and then give some reasons for your choice.

4. Write a short story set in a magical world of witches, wizards and fairies. Think carefully about:

- interesting characters (heroes and enemies)
- magical settings
- strange powers and potions
- a battle between good and evil
- a happy ending

Learning about language

Verbs (doing words)

Verbs, also known as doing words, tell us the action that is taking place in a sentence.

Look at this line, taken from *A witch's song*:

Boil *their bones and* **fry** *their skin.*

This sentence contains two verbs, **boil** and **fry**. Every sentence needs at least one verb. Here are two more sentences, this time from the second passage:

Old wise women sometimes **granted** *wishes as a reward to kind children who had* **helped** *them.*

Fairies often **gave** *three wishes to people they* **liked**.

Verbs are doing words because they show us what is being done. In the first example, the old wise women are **granting** wishes because the children had **helped** them. In the second example, the fairies are doing the **giving** to people whom they **liked**. These are all actions, so the words underlined are verbs.

Remember: verbs do not have to be physical actions, like **kick** a ball, or **jump** in the air. Verbs like **think**, **say** or **remember** are just as important. Verbs have different endings such as **-ed**, **-s** or **-ing** depending on how they are used.

Exercise 3.4

Write these sentences. Underline the verb(s) in each one. Look for the actions that are being performed by someone. What are the people actually *doing*?

1. The witches cast a spell on the children and turned them into mice.

2. The teachers stood on the desks and shouted.

3. One child thought he was growing fur.

4. If you see a wishing well, throw a coin in.

5. The fairies and dwarves lived deep underground.

6. I met a dragon king and he gave me a wonderful gift.

Exercise 3.5

Fill in the gaps in these sentences with a suitable verb from the words below:

broke   running   climbing   shouted   touch

made   turned   hanging   blow

1. The witches all ———— 'HOORAY!'

2. The children ———— into mice.

3. Mice were ———— around the schoolroom floor.

4. ———— the object of your spell or ———— on it gently.

5. We ———— the wish-bone and I ———— a wish.

6. You can reach it by ———— a rope or a ladder ———— down from the clouds.

Making a sentence

You need several important ingredients to make a sentence:

- a capital letter
- a subject
- a verb
- a full stop at the end

For example: *The wicked witches   laughed.*
                        subject   verb

The **subject** in every sentence is the person or thing that is **doing** the action. In this example, the wicked witches are doing the laughing, so they are the subject.

The sentence begins with a capital **T** for 'The' and finishes with a **full stop**, to show that we have reached the end.

A sentence is a group of words that work together to make sense. Without a verb, or without a subject, the sentence would not make sense. For example,

The wicked witches.

or

The laughed.

You may be asking 'The wicked witches did what?' for the first example, or 'Who laughed?' for the second one. We need to have all the correct information to make a proper sentence.

Exercise 3.6

Which of these are proper sentences? Copy out each line and then put a tick (✓) to show it is a sentence or a cross (X) if you think it is unfinished. Remember, you need **all** the ingredients to make a sentence.

1. The witch danced.

2. The cauldron

3. I cried.

4. The dragon kings

5. lies deep below the ground.

6. give you a wonderful gift

Exercise 3.7

Write these sentences. Then underline the subject in red and the verb in green.

1. The witch waved her wand.

2. The wizard stirred the potion.

3. The mice scurried away.

4. I threw a coin in the wishing well.

5. Deep underground the fairies danced.

6. A dragon flew past my window.

Can you spell?

Rhyming words

Look again at the following pairs of lines from *A witch's song*.

Offer chocs vith magic **powder**!
Say 'Eat up!' then say it **louder**.

A boy who's standing next to **her**
Screams, 'Help! I think I'm growing **fur**!'

Notice how the lines of poetry end with words that rhyme – **powder/louder** and **her/fur**.

Rhyming is a technique that many poets use to make their poems lively and interesting when read aloud.

Finding words that rhyme is sometimes easy...

sat – cat   sign – line   thought – caught

... and sometimes a little harder:

guided – decided   Hungary – ironmongery   doughnut – throw nuts

Putting rhyming words together is only the first step.
Next you have to know how to spell them, so always have a
dictionary or thesaurus handy. Words which rhyme sound
the same but they are often spelled differently.

Exercise 3.8

Can you think of two rhyming words for each of these words? Write out each one and then put the rhyming words next to it. Use a dictionary to check the spelling of tricky words. Remember it is the **sound** which has to match. The spelling may be different.

For example: *Dad – glad, sad*

1. table
2. witch
3. girl
4. run
5. school
6. book
7. address
8. soil
9. hour
10. game

Exercise 3.9

The following words contains ten sets of rhyming pairs. Match up the rhyming words and write them out in pairs. Be careful to spell each one correctly.

part	plain	swimming	small	worry
treat	bough	heart	find	eight
brimming	fall	cow	sweet	naught
behind	hurry	sort	Kate	train

Speaking and listening

1. In pairs, role-play a conversation between two children: one child has just returned from a walk in the forest, where he or she is sure there was a fairy, dancing between the trees. The other child does not believe this story. Will he or she be persuaded?

2. Working in a small group, practise reading *A witch's song* aloud, taking a few lines each to learn off by heart. Try to put some interesting actions to the poem, and remember to use lots of expression when you perform it.

3. Have a class discussion in which you share your answers to the following questions: Are there really such things as witches and wizards? Can people have special powers? What do you think?

4. Sit in a circle with your classmates. Begin narrating a ghost story, in which each person in the circle takes a turn to make up the next line of the story. You could begin with these lines: *Suddenly the great oak door behind us slammed shut, plunging the room into darkness. I knew we should never have come...*

Have you read?

Here are some stories of witches, wizards and magical worlds:

The Witch's Dog by Frank Rodgers (Puffin Books)
The Worst Witch by Jill Murphy (Puffin Books)
Harry Potter and the Philosopher's Stone by J. K. Rowling (Bloomsbury)
Lauren the Puppy Fairy (Rainbow Magic) by Daisy Meadows (Orchard Books)
Fairy Tales by Terry Jones & Michael Foreman (Puffin Books)
The Fly-by-night by Terry Jones & Michael Foreman (Ramboro Books)
Gobbolino the Witch's Cat by Ursula Moray Williams (Kingfisher Books)
The Wizard of Oz and the Magic Merry-Go-Round
by Roger S. Baum (Overmountain Press)

Other things to do...

- Create your own recipe book full of magic potions. Invent some extraordinary mixtures for amazing spells. Don't forget to include some unusual ingredients in each recipe. Remember: don't try making these at home (and definitely DO NOT drink them!).

- If you could have three wishes, what would they be, and why? Think about this for a few moments, make some notes and then share your thoughts with the class. You may find others have the same wishes too.

- Everybody has heard of Harry Potter and Hogwarts, the school for wizards. But what if you could really go to such a school? Would you enjoy it? Write an imaginary diary for the first week at wizard school. What have you been up to? Are you enjoying it? How is it different from ordinary school?

Chapter 4

Buried treasure

Long John Silver and his band of ruthless pirates are searching for buried treasure. Young Jim Hawkins, the hero of this story, is with them. But Dr Livesey and Ben Gunn are on their trail…

The chart said the treasure was buried beneath a tall tree on Mizzenmast Hill. As the pirates climbed the hill they argued about which tree it could be.

5   Suddenly one of the pirates yelled. The others ran over to him. There, at the foot of a tree, lay a human skeleton which was pointing towards the top of the hill.

The pirates stared at it in silence. Then they heard a strange, high voice: 'Fifteen men on the dead man's chest,' it sang.

The pirates were terrified.

10   'It's Flint's ghost,' they gasped.

'It's only someone trying to scare us,' Long John said calmly.

The pirates struggled on up the hill. At last they saw a tall tree in front of them. They charged towards it, then stopped in their tracks.

A huge hole had been dug at the foot of the tree. Someone had got there
15   before the pirates and all of the treasure had gone.

Long John secretly gave Jim a pistol. 'Stand by for trouble,' he whispered.

The pirates jumped into the hole and began digging. One of them held up a coin. 'Did we come all this way just for this?' he roared, as he climbed out of the hole. 'Down with Long John,' he said.

20   Suddenly shots rang out from the bushes and two of the pirates dropped dead.

The next minute Dr Livesey and Ben Gunn rushed into the clearing, their guns smoking. The three pirates still alive ran away.

'Quick,' cried Dr Livesey. 'We must head them off before they reach
25   the boats.'

They charged down the hill with Long John Silver hobbling along behind them. They reached the beach before the pirates, knocked a hole in one boat and pushed out to sea in the other.

(From Robert Louis Stevenson's Treasure Island, retold by Angela Wilkes, 1982)

Exercise 4.1

Read the passage from *Treasure Island*. Then answer the following questions in proper sentences.

1. Where was the treasure buried, according to the chart?

2. What made one of the pirates yell?

3. (a) When the pirates heard a strange voice singing, who did they think it was?
    (b) How did Long John Silver calm them down?

4. Why did Long John suspect there was going to be trouble? What did he think was about to happen, and why?

5. Who shot the pirates?

6. How did Jim and his rescuers make sure the pirates would not follow them as they escaped? What did they do?

7. Write down dictionary definitions for the following words: (a) *chart* (line 1); (b) *pirates* (line 2); (c) *skeleton* (line 5); (d) *pistol* (line 16).

How to make a treasure map

In stories, old maps of desert islands help people to find buried treasure. Make your own treasure map for a fantasy island.

You will need:
- paper
5 - poster paints
- paintbrush
- pencil
- ruler
- felt-tip pens
10 - scissors

1. Scrunch a piece of paper into a loose ball. Then flatten it out with your hands.

2. Dilute some green or brown paint to make it very watery. Paint a wash over the whole sheet of crumpled paper. Leave to dry.

15 3. Draw a grid of squares over the paper with a pencil and ruler. Each line should be the same distance apart.

4. Draw the outline of a desert island. Make it an interesting, unusual shape. Add some waves to show where the sea is.

5. Draw some pictures on your map to stand for different things such as
20 lakes and volcanoes. Make the symbols small and simple.

6. Draw a key to explain your symbols and add a north arrow. Shade the edges to make the map look old.

(From Maps and Mapping by Deborah Chancellor, 2006)

Exercise 4.2

Read the instructions for 'How to make a treasure map'. Then answer the following questions in proper sentences.

1. Why do you think you should scrunch a piece of paper into a ball first? What effect would this have on the map that you make?

2. How would readers be able to see which part is land and which part is the sea on your treasure map?

3. What natural features does the writer suggest you put on your treasure island?

4. Write two verbs that give you instructions in this passage.

5. Explain in your own words what a map key is.

6. Use a dictionary to find the meanings of these words: (a) *scrunch* (line 11); (b) *dilute* (line 13); (c) *outline* (line 17); (d) *symbols* (line 20).

Exercise 4.3

Your turn to write:

1. Write your own short story set on a desert island in the middle of the ocean, which, according to legend, hides some buried treasure. Who will find it first in your story – the heroes or the villains?

2. Read the passage *Buried treasure* again. Imagine you are one of the pirates. Retell this story scene from the pirate's point of view. Remember to write in the first person (I/me) and describe how you felt when you heard the ghostly singing, and when you discovered that the treasure had gone.

3. What would be the most amazing treasure you might find buried in your garden? Write a few sentences describing this treasure. Why is it so special?

4. Think about your journey to school. Write down a set of instructions to help someone find the school from your house. Then draw a sketch map of the journey. Try to include some of the important landmarks you pass on the way.

Learning about language

Story speech

When characters speak to one another in stories, the words they say are surrounded by **speech marks** (" ") so that readers can picture what they are saying, as they say it. This is how characters come to life in stories.

Speech marks can be **double** (" and ") or **single** (' and ').

Look at this example of story speech from *Treasure Island*:

'It's Flint's ghost,' they gasped.

We can see exactly what the pirates said, when they heard the ghostly singing, because their words are separated from the rest of the sentence (**they gasped**) by speech marks.

Speech marks are sometimes called **inverted commas** because they look like commas upside down.

When writing story speech, always include some punctuation at the end of the spoken words **before** the final speech mark.

Story speech can end in the following ways:

- a **comma** (if it ends half way through the sentence):
  'Let's look here for the treasure,' suggested Long John.

- a **full stop** (if it finishes the sentence):
  Jim said, 'I think I can hear footsteps.'

- an **exclamation mark** (if the speaker is exclaiming something, or shouting):
  'It's all gone!' cried the pirates.

- or a **question mark** (if the speaker is asking a question):
  'Where is the treasure?' said Jim.

Remember: in all these examples, the final speech mark comes **after** the punctuation.

Exercise 4.4

Rewrite these sentences, putting speech marks around the actual words spoken.

1. We'll be rich! cried the girls, as they began to dig for treasure.

2. Do you think this island feels spooky? said David.

3. There's treasure in my garden, declared little Edward.

4. Land ahoy! cried the sailor.

5. Mary smiled and said When I'm older I'm going to be a pirate.

Exercise 4.5 ✏️

Write out these sentences placing a comma, full stop, exclamation mark or question mark at the end of the story speech.

For example: *'Help' cried the sailor.* becomes *'Help!' cried the sailor.*

1. The pirates asked 'Where is the treasure'

2. 'Look what you've done to my boat' shouted Long John Silver.

3. 'I'm glad you rescued me' said Jim.

4. 'Why did you join the pirates' Dr Livesey enquired.

5. Ben Gunn said 'I know where the treasure is'

Verbs to instruct

Look at the following sentences, taken from the treasure map instructions:

1. *Scrunch a piece of paper into a loose ball. Flatten it out again with your hands.*

2. *Dilute some green or brown paint to make it very watery. Paint a wash over the whole sheet of crumpled paper. Leave to dry.*

3. *Draw a grid of squares over the paper with a pencil and ruler. Each line should be the same distance apart.*

The word in blue in each sentence gives you an **instruction** or **command**. It tells you what to do. To make the treasure map you will need to **scrunch**, **dilute** and **draw**. These are all actions, so these words are **verbs**. But each of them is a special type of verb called an **imperative**.

You will find lots of imperatives in other types of instructions, including:

recipes:	*stir, whisk, beat*
directions:	*turn, proceed, take, stop*
building instructions:	*fit, hammer, screw, bend, slide*

In this book we often instruct you to **read**, **write** or **think**.

Exercise 4.6

Write out these sentences, filling in the gaps with the right imperative from the words below:

   take   draw   place   turn   walk   whisk

1. At the end of the road —————— right.

2. —————— the egg whites until they become light and fluffy.

3. —————— the cake on a baking tray and cook for forty minutes.

4. To make the map, —————— the shape of an island in the middle of the paper.

5. After the church, —————— the second road on the right.

6. To find the treasure, —————— twenty paces east and then five paces west.

Exercise 4.7

Think of an interesting sentence for each of the following imperatives. Remember these are to be used as instructions to the reader.

1. take
2. press
3. telephone
4. cut
5. cook

6. fold
7. mix
8. turn
9. slice
10. install

Can you spell?

Silent letters

Look again at the word **island** in Robert Louis Stevenson's *Treasure Island*. Say the word out loud... *island*.

Can you hear every letter? The answer is you can hear every one except for the **s**. This is a silent s.

There are many words that contain silent letters. It is easy to forget that the silent letters are there because you cannot hear them. But this could lead to spelling mistakes. Look at these examples:

knee   *comb*   *gnome*

Can you identify which letters are not pronounced when you say these words aloud? The answers are:

knee (silent **k**)   *comb* (silent **b**)   *gnome* (silent **g**)

There is no rule to tell you which letters will be silent. It depends on the word. But there are some common letter patterns worth remembering, like these:

kn-   *knock, knee*
sch-   *school, scheme*
gn-   *gnome, reign*
-mb   *bomb, climb*
wh-   *white, where*
gu-   *guest, guard*
-st-   *listen, hustle*

Exercise 4.8

Copy these sentences into your book. Each one contains a word containing a silent letter. Circle this word and then underline the actual letter which is silent.

For example: *The visitor knocked on the door.*
          The visitor k̲nocked on the door.

1. We tied a knot in the rope.

2. When I leave school, I should like to be a pilot.

3. The lamb was small and cuddly.

4. I saw a sign to London.

5. I found a splinter in my thumb.

6. The dog gnawed on his juicy bone.

Exercise 4.9

Write an appropriate sentence for each of these words. Then underline the silent letter in each one.

For example: *guard – There was a guard at the gate.*

1. glisten
2. guinea-pig
3. why
4. tomb
5. know
6. wrap

Speaking and listening

1. Take turns to be one of the pirates from the *Treasure Island* passage. Sit in the hot seat at the front of the class. Answer questions on how you felt when you thought you could be rich, and then how you felt when you realised that the treasure had already been taken.

2. Think again about how instructions are put together. Look back at the example of how to make a treasure map. Think about the numbered tasks, each one beginning with an imperative verb. Choose a simple task (like brushing your teeth, tying your shoelaces or riding your bike). Then imagine you had to instruct someone how to do this using **spoken** words rather than writing it down. Try it out with a friend.

3. Working in small groups, act out the scene from *Treasure Island* when Long John Silver and his pirates find that the treasure has gone. What happens next? Perform your scene for the class. Think particularly about the expressions on the pirates' faces.

4. Find out more about pirates. Are there still pirates today? Once you have collected some information, from books, magazines and the Internet, share what you have learned by putting together a class talk, with a friend. You could begin by talking about Long John Silver.

Have you read?

Here are some stories and activity books about pirates and buried treasure:

Pandora the Pirate Princess by Judy Brown (Simon & Schuster Children's Books)
Pirate Adventures by Russell Punter (Usborne Publishing)
The Birthday Bash (Pirate School) by Jeremy Strong (Puffin Books)
The Search for Sunken Treasure by Geronimo Stilton (Scholastic)
Backbeard: Pirate for Hire by Matthew McEligott (Walker & Company)
The Night Pirates by Peter Harris (Egmont Books)
Mrs Pepperpot and the Treasure by Alf Proysen (Red Fox)
Pirate Things to Make and Do by Rebecca Gilpin (Usborne Publishing)
Pirate Ship Sticker Activity Book by Steven James Petruccio (Dover Publications)

Other things to do...

- Find out more about the famous story of *Treasure Island*. There have been several story versions and many films of this great tale by Robert Louis Stevenson. See what you can find out about it and then share your information with the class. Use the Internet, books and encylopaedias.

- Make a bigger treasure map, by following the same instructions, but using larger paper. Draw a really interesting treasure island, with lots of land features, all with scary names, like *Devil's Mountain*, *Whispering Woods* and *Old Jack's Grave*.

- What do pirates wear? What sort of clothes do they have? What do they carry with them? How do they protect themselves? Draw a design for a pirate costume, complete with clothes, belongings and weapons. Then label what you have drawn.

Chapter 5

The diary of a young Roman girl

Secundia Fulvia Popillia is writing about her life in Rome, in the summer of the year we now call 74 AD.

I know for sure that a divine miracle occurred today, though nobody else knows but me. I asked the goddess Vesta herself for help, and I think I got it. It began with a journey in our litter for Mother, Cecilia and me, right across the heart of Rome, through the Forum towards the Temple of
5 Vesta. The Forum is always so exciting! It would be hard to imagine the grandness of it without seeing it – the huge space, such important buildings all around it, such grand statues, and so very many people.

At one point we had to stop and wait to let a fat snooty-looking senator pass, surrounded by his guards. Then we nearly bumped into a man
10 reading poetry out loud, and I felt quite dizzy after our bearers had to weave their way through several bunches of out-of-town tourists gawping at the statues. I'll bet one or two pickpockets stood behind them, though they'd be too fast to spot.

Eventually we came in sight of the Temple, smothered in marble and
15 columns. What makes it really easy to spot amongst the other temples is the smoke curling up through a hole in the circular roof from the sacred fire kept burning below to please the goddess.

Livia was already inside, as were Julia and a very excited Cornelia. It was cool, and smelt so strongly of incense my eyes began to smart.
20 There were murmurs and the rustling of ladies' long tunics as they brushed the floor. Because it was the middle of the Vestalia Festival it was a busy day, with lots of respectable ladies visiting to pay homage to the goddess and so help to ensure happiness at home. (No men, of course. They're not allowed!)

25 Cornelia pointed out an enclosure that she said was the room holding the Temple's sacred objects. 'If only we could see them,' she sighed longingly. But to do that we would have to be married and then turn up on the one day of the year they open the room.

'What are the sacred objects?' I whispered back.

30   'I don't know! Some kind of statues, I think. They're secret! she replied. 'Oh look!'

Suddenly a Vestal Virgin appeared in a white dress, looking very proud and tall because of her high bridal hairstyle. She moved towards the sacred fire and looked as if she was splashing liquid on the floor from a flask.

35   'What's she doing?' I asked Cornelia.

'She's pouring a libation, an offering to make the goddess happy. Now will be a good time to ask for her blessing,' Cornelia suggested.

So I did, silently. I asked her for good fortune, and a little extra help for the Fulvius family.

(From History Diaries: The Diary of a Young Roman Girl by Moira Butterfield, 2003)

Exercise 5.1 ✏️

Read the passage from *The diary of a young Roman girl*. Then answer these questions in proper sentences.

1. What two features of the Forum in Rome make it seem so grand?

2. What was the first thing Secundia and her companions had to stop for as they crossed the Forum?

3. What makes the Temple of Vesta stand out from the other temples?

4. What made the writer's eyes water inside the temple?

5. Why was it a particularly busy day in the Temple of Vesta?

6. Do you think the young Roman girl believes in gods and goddesses? Write a few sentences to explain what you think, and why.

7. Give the meanings of the following words. You may use a dictionary.
   (a) *divine* (line 1); (b) *forum* (line 4); (c) *gawping* (line 11);
   (d) *sacred* (line 16).

• •

Roman words

Do you recognise any of these words? See how they are presented in alphabetical order. This type of text is called a **glossary**.

Aqueduct	A man-made channel designed to bring clean water to Roman towns.
Barbarian	The name given to all those who lived beyond the Roman <u>empire</u>. The Romans believed that Barbarians were uncivilised, violent people.
Boudicca	A famous tribal queen in Britain, who fought against the Romans.
Caesar, Julius	A famous Roman general. He was born in about 100 BC and was killed in 44 BC.
Celts	A group of people who were living in France and Great Britain when the Romans invaded.

5 (line number beside Barbarian)

10 (line number beside Celts)

	Centurion	A Roman commander, in charge of 100 <u>legionaries</u>.
	Claudius	A Roman <u>emperor</u> who ruled Rome from AD 41 to AD 54. Claudius made Britain a province of the Roman empire.
15	Emperor	The ruler of an <u>empire</u>.
	Empire	A large area made up of different countries, but ruled by a single <u>emperor</u>.
	Forum	A large space (surrounded by important buildings) in the centre of a Roman town. Used for holding markets.
20	Hadrian	Roman <u>emperor</u> between the years AD 117 and AD 138.
	Hadrian's Wall	A wall built in England by the Romans to keep the Barbarians of Scotland away. It was 73 miles long and named after the emperor Hadrian.
	Legion	A group of about 5000 soldiers in the Roman army.
25	Legionaries	A Roman soldier – a member of a <u>legion</u> in the Roman army.
	Romans	People who created a vast <u>empire</u> across the world, led from the city of Rome over 2000 years ago. They had one of the biggest <u>empires</u> the world has ever seen.
30	Senator	A member of the Senate, Rome's governing council.
	Villa	A large Roman house and garden.

(By Andrew Hammond, 2007)

Exercise 5.2 ✏️

Read the glossary of Roman words. Then answer these questions in proper sentences.

1. (a) What was the name the Romans gave to people who lived outside their empire?

   (b) What did they think these people were like?

2. When was Julius Caesar killed?

3. How many legionaries would a centurion lead?

4. What might you find in a forum?

5. What is the name for a member of Rome's leading council?

6. Write dictionary definitions for these words: (a) *uncivilised* (line 5); (b) *invaded* (line 11); (c) *governing* (line 30); (d) *council* (line 30).

Exercise 5.3

Your turn to write:

1. What do you know about the Romans? Write a short information book containing some interesting facts, sketches and pictures of the Romans and their empire. You could begin with some information found in the glossary. Use books, magazines and Internet sites.

2. Write part of your own 'Diary of a young Roman girl (or boy).' What other things could you do in Roman times? Why not describe the villa where you live, or the great Colosseum, where you might see gladiators fight.

3. Rome is the capital city of Italy and very famous. But London, capital of the UK, is a world-famous city too. What do you know about it? Using books, atlases and Internet sites, prepare a 'factfile' for London, with interesting information about its population, size, location, important buildings, famous residents, historical events, etc.

4. Find some more interesting words to add to the Roman glossary. For each word, write a short explanation of what it means, and any other interesting information you can find about it. You may have lots of books about the Romans in your school library.

Learning about language

First or third person

When we write out a verb in English (or French, Latin or any other language), we list it like this:

	English	Latin	French
1st person singular	I love	amo	j'aime
2nd person singular	you love	amas	tu aimes
3rd person singular	he/she/it loves	amat	il/elle aime
1st person plural	we love	amamus	nous aimons
2nd person plural	you love	amatis	vous aimez
3rd person plural	they love	amant	ils/elles aiment

So, the phrase **first or third person** means the person who is performing the action in a sentence – the word that comes just before the verb. For example, it might be:

I run to the shop.

or

He runs to the shop.

In the first sentence, it is 'I' who am running to the shop. This is using the **first person narrative**.

The second sentence uses the **third person narrative**, which is 'he', 'she' or 'it'.

Think about the stories you like to read. Are they written in the **first** or **third** person? Are you reading the story from the writer's own viewpoint (first person 'I') or is the writer telling you about what happened to someone else (third person 'he, she, it')?

The diary of a young Roman girl is written in the first person. For example,

'I felt quite dizzy…'

If this was written in the third person, it would become:

She felt quite dizzy…

A diary is usually written in the first person – because it is an account of what happened to the writer, in his or her **own** words.

When you write stories, think carefully about whether you are going to choose to write in the first person (**I** woke up) or the third person (**he**, **she** or **it** woke up). Then you must be sure to keep to the same all the way through.

The first and third person narratives both have plurals too. The following table shows how verbs can be written in the first or third person, singular or plural:

Verb	First person		Third person	
	Singular	Plural	Singular	Plural
to run	I run	we run	he run**s**	they run
to dance	I dance	we dance	she danc**es**	they dance
to cry	I cry	we cry	it cr**ies**	they cry

Exercise 5.4

Copy this table into your book and then fill in the spaces. You can use *he*, *she* or *it* for the third person singular.

Verb	First person		Third person	
	Singular	Plural	Singular	Plural
to laugh	I laugh		he laughs	
to rise		we rise		they rise
to stay	I stay		he stays	
		we taste		they taste
to dry		we dry		
			she cares	
	I catch			

Exercise 5.5 ✏️

Rewrite these sentences in the first person. Remember to check if it is singular or plural.

e.g. *He opens the box.*   *I open the box.*

1. They enter the cinema.

2. She dances on ice.

3. It falls over.

4. They eat chocolate cake.

5. On a rainy day, she likes to splash in puddles.

6. After the match, they celebrate in style.

Personal pronouns

Pronouns are words that replace nouns. They are used to avoid repeating the same noun several times.

Jane asked Tom if Tom would like to accompany Jane to the cinema…

This sentence sounds clumsy because the nouns Tom and Jane are repeated. With the help of some pronouns, we can change it to:

*Jane asked Tom if **he** would like to accompany **her** to the cinema…*

This sounds much better. The pronouns used are called **personal pronouns**. Like all pronouns, these can be singular or plural. They can also be divided into **first**, **second** or **third** person. The first and third person you will recognise from the previous section (**I** and **he**). The second person refers to **you**.

	Singular	Plural
First person	I/me	we/us
Second person	you	you
Third person	he/him, she/her, it	they/them

Exercise 5.6

Rewrite these sentences replacing the repeated noun each time with the correct personal pronoun from the words below. Then underline it. Look at the example below:

e.g.   *Mum asked, 'Jeremy, would Jeremy like more rice pudding?'*
Mum asked, 'Jeremy, would <u>you</u> like more rice pudding?'

   them   he   we   you   they   us

1.   Gregg said that Gregg felt better now.

2.   The players believed the players could win the game.

3.   Andie's parents said, 'Andie's parents would be delighted to come.'

4.   'Would Bevan like to go fishing, Bevan?' asked Tom.

5.   The queen drove past the crowds and gave the crowds a wave.

6.   Nikki and Petra said, 'Can you pick Nikki and Petra up at five o'clock?'

Exercise 5.7

Remember that the pronoun refers to the noun it is replacing. Copy out these sentences, filling in the correct pronoun from the choice in brackets at the end.

1.   When Tim arrived at school, ———— realised he had forgotten his bag. (he/she/it)

2.   My parents told me, '———— are very proud of you!' (I/We)

3.   Emma was delighted when ———— was given an A grade for her work. (he/she/it)

4.   Amil and Yoseph always shared jokes as ———— walked to school. (you/they)

5.   The aeroplane circled the airport for a few minutes before ———— landed. (he/she/it)

6.   Anzar asked, 'Would ———— like to go swimming on Saturday, Peter?' (I/you)

Can you spell?

Alphabetical lists

Some books and texts, like the Roman glossary above, present words in alphabetical order. This is so that you can look up a word you need quickly and simply, by thinking about the letter it begins with. Dictionaries and thesauruses are arranged in this way.

Look at this section from the Roman glossary of words.

Aqueduct A man-made channel designed to bring clean water to Roman towns.

Barbarian The name given to all those who lived beyond the Roman <u>empire</u>. The Romans believed that Barbarians were uncivilised, violent people.

Boudicca A famous tribal queen in Britain, who fought against the Romans.

Caesar, Julius A famous Roman general. He was born in about 100 BC and was killed in 44 BC.

The main words on the left go down in **alphabetical order**. *Aqueduct* is first because it begins with 'A'. *Barbarian* is next because it begins with 'B'. The word, *Boudicca* also begins with 'B' but its second letter is 'o'. The second letter of *Barbarian* is 'a', which comes before 'o' in the alphabet, so *Barbarian* comes before *Boudicca* in the glossary.

When listing (or looking for) words alphabetically, if two words have the same first letter, then look at the second letter, then the third, and so on.

Exercise 5.8

Put these names in alphabetical order.

Joseph	Mark	Daphne
Emily	Elizabeth	James
Hassan	Michael	Yolanda
Edward	Andrew	Alexandra

Exercise 5.9

These words are taken from *The diary of a young Roman girl*. Look them up in a dictionary, then copy them out, **with their meanings**, into your book in alphabetical order.

journey	tunic	fire
statue	flask	miracle
temple	secret	
sacred	murmur	

Speaking and listening

1. Take turns to sit in the 'hot seat' at the front of the classroom and answer questions in the role of Popilla, the young Roman girl in the passage above (or you can be a young Roman boy). Questioners could ask you how you feel, what you do in Rome and what you would like to be when you are older.

2. Play a game of word tennis. Sit opposite a partner and take turns to call out words that are connected to the subject of the Romans – e.g. forum, villa, empire. One person wins a point when the other makes a mistake by repeating a word already said or hestitating and saying 'erm'!

3. Put together a presentation or class talk on one particular aspect of Rome or the Romans. You could choose: the Roman army, Roman houses, the city of Rome, gladiators, Julius Caesar or the Romans in Britain, for example.

4. Working in small groups, act out what happens in the scene from *The diary of a young Roman girl*. Read it through again and think about how many characters you will need and what everyone does. Don't forget that snooty-looking senator.

Have you read?

Here are some stories and information books about the Romans:

Clottus and the Ghostly Gladiator by Ann Jungman (A & C Black)
Bacillus and the Beastly Bath by Ann Jungman (A & C Black)
The Rotten Romans (Horrible Histories) by Terry Deary (Scholastic Hippo)
The Ruthless Romans (Horrible Histories) by Terry Deary (Scholastic Hippo)
Romans by Katie Daynes (Usborne Publishing)
Conquering Romans (Know-it-all Guides) by Nigel Crowle (Puffin Books)
The Romans by Sally Hewitt (Franklin Watts Ltd)
Roman Aromas (Smelly Old History) by Mary J. Dobson (Oxford University Press)

PERFECT STORM
THE SNOWMAN

Other things to do...

*   Find out more about Hadrian's Wall. How much of it is still standing today? Use books, atlases and Internet sites to find information and then share it with your class or at home.

*   Write a story in which you are living in Britain when the Romans invade. What happens? How will your life change forever? What are the good things and the bad things that the Romans bring with them?

*   Make your own **illustrated** glossary of Roman words. Choose about ten words – different from those in the Roman Glossary above – and then write some information for each one. You could include some lovely drawings too.

Chapter 6

Good Company

I sleep in a room at the top of a house
With a flea, and a fly, and a soft-scratching mouse,
And a spider that hangs by a thread from the ceiling,
Who gives me each day such a curious feeling
5 When I watch him at work on the beautiful weave
Of his web that's so fine I can hardly believe
It won't all end up in such a terrible tangle,
For he sways as he weaves, and spins as he dangles.
I cannot get up to that spider, I know,
10 And I hope he won't get down to me here below,
And yet when I awake in the chill morning air
I'd miss him if he were not still swinging there,
For I have in my room such good company,
There's him, and the mouse, and the fly, and the flea.

(By Leonard Clark, in Classic Poems to Read Aloud selected by James Berry, 1997)

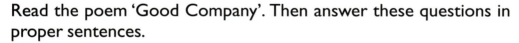

Exercise 6.1

Read the poem 'Good Company'. Then answer these questions in proper sentences.

1. With how many creatures does the writer share his room?

2. What is it about the spider that makes the poet so curious?

3. The poet has chosen to call his poem 'Good Company'. Do you think this is a good name? What do you think it is referring to?

4. What sort of mood does this poem create – friendly, cosy, scary? Write a sentence or two to describe the mood of this poem and how it makes you feel.

5. Look for a rhyming pattern in the poem and then explain how the pattern works.

6. Find meanings for the following words. You may use a dictionary.
(a) *thread* (line 3); (b) *curious* (line 4); (c) *weave* (line 5);
(d) *dangles* (line 8).

King of the insects

Beetles

If you pick an insect at random, there is a good chance that it will be a
beetle. That is because beetles are the most successful insects on Earth.
So far, scientists have identified nearly 400 000 different species – some
5 are only just visible to the naked eye, while others are as big as an adult's
hand. Adult beetles have extra-tough bodies and strong legs, but their
most important feature is their hardened forewings, which fit over their
hindwings like a case. With this special protection, they can clamber about
in all kinds of places to search for food.

10 ### Gentle giant

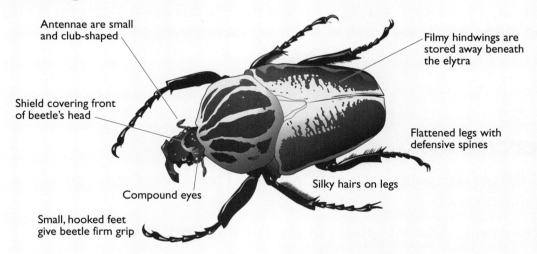

Antennae are small
and club-shaped

Filmy hindwings are
stored away beneath
the elytra

Shield covering front
of beetle's head

Flattened legs with
defensive spines

Silky hairs on legs

Compound eyes

Small, hooked feet
give beetle firm grip

Weighing up to 100g (4oz) – about three times as much as a mouse –
Goliath beetles are the heaviest insects in the world. Like most beetles,
these tropical monsters have hardened forewings, called elytra, which
protect the more delicate hindwings. When a beetle flies, the elytra open
15 up, but only the hindwings beat. Goliath beetles feed on forest flowers, and
have small heads with stubby mouthparts. They have strong legs that end
in hooked feet.

Beetle colours

Many beetles are jet black, but some have
20 eye-catching colours. The tropical leaf beetle,
from Southeast Asia, is iridescent, with a
beautiful metallic sheen. Some scarab beetles
glisten like pieces of gold, while many smaller
beetles have bright stripes or spots, warning
25 predators that they are dangerous to eat.
Wasp beetles have a bold yellow and black
pattern – a colour scheme that makes other
animals think they can sting.

Scavenging beetle

30 The churchyard beetle is a typical scavenger, coming out to feed after
dark. It lives on the dead remains of animals and plants, and also on any
small live animals that come its way. Scavenging beetles clear up all kinds
of natural waste, which helps to break down nutrients, so they can be
used by plants again and again. These beetles can cause problems if they
35 get indoors, because some of them eat stored food.

(From e.explore: Insect by David Burnie, 2005)

Exercise 6.2

Read the passage entitled *King of the insects*. Then answer these questions in
proper sentences.

1. How many different species of beetle have scientists found so far?

2. (a) What are beetles' most important feature?

    (b) How are they important? What do they do?

3. On Goliath beetles, these special features have a particular name.
    What is it?

4. Which type of beetle glistens like gold?

5. How do some smaller beetles discourage predators from eating them?

6. Why would you not want a scavenging beetle indoors?

7. Find dictionary definitions for the following words: (a) *visible* (line 5); (b) *hardened* (line 7); (c) *delicate* (line 14); (d) *predators* (line 25).

Exercise 6.3

Your turn to write:

1. Write a poem of your own about an insect. Choose one you like very much or strongly dislike. It might be a spider, a beetle or a beautiful butterfly. Try to think about how this insect makes you *feel*. Use lots of interesting adjectives. You might try to make your poem rhyme too.

2. What might your house look like if you were a fly or a beetle? Imagine all that enormous furniture and those giants' shoes stamping about the place. Write a short description of your house (or a room) from the insect's point of view. Use the first person (I/me).

3. Find out more about the amazing world of insects. You could use information books and Internet sites. Then put together your own information book on a particular type of insect. Include some writing, sketches and labelled diagrams.

4. Put together your own wordsearch, containing lots of insect names. Start with a grid (about ten squares wide and ten squares tall). Write out your insect names in different directions across the grid. Then hide the names by placing lots of other letters around them.

Learning about language

Ending a sentence

Every sentence needs to have a clear ending. Readers need to know that the sentence has finished and it is time to move onto something else.

A sentence can end in three different ways. You can use:

a **full stop** (.)

a **question mark** (?)

or **an exclamation mark** (!)

As you will remember from Chapter 2, a **full stop** is the most common way of ending a sentence. It shows the reader when to pause, take a breath and then move onto the next sentence. Look back at the full stops used in this paragraph.

Without full stops (and capital letters), writing would look very strange indeed, and the reader would not be able to make sense of what is written down.

As you might expect, a **question mark** is used when the sentence asks a question:

Would you like some chocolate cake?
Is it raining in England?
Are we nearly there yet?

Of course the question mark still contains a full stop, with a squiggle above it. It is as powerful as a full stop – it shows that the sentence has ended. It also shows the reader that an answer is needed.

An **exclamation mark** is perhaps the most powerful of all the punctuation marks. That is why you shouldn't use it too often. It helps the sentence that it follows to have a big **impact** on the reader, either because it is funny, or because the writer is feeling surprised, angry, impressed or frightened. For example:

Wow! I wasn't expecting that!
How dare you!
What a fabulous story you've written!
Help! It's a ghost!

Exclamation marks are often used in story speech, to show the strong feelings of the characters speaking, or to suggest that they are shouting. They are used much less often in other forms of writing.

Beware: too many exclamation marks can cause them to lose their impact. So just save them for special occasions.

Exercise 6.4

Decide whether these sentences need to end in a full stop, question mark or exclamation mark. Then copy out each one into your book, with the correct ending.

1. What is the weather like in Spain—

2. Mum shouted, 'Get down from there—

3. Kick-off will be at three o'clock—

4. Mrs Jackson smiled and said, 'What a beautiful painting—

5. Would you like mashed potatoes or chips—

6. The train leaves in twenty minutes—

Exercise 6.5

Write four sentences of your own using the following endings:

1. full stop

2. question mark

3. exclamation mark to show anger

4. exclamation mark to show surprise

Alliteration

Look at the following pairs of words from the two passages above.

terrible tangle
Gentle **G**iants

The words in each pair begin with the same sound. This is called **alliteration** and it is a technique used by lots of writers to make their writing fun to read. Words that begin with the same letters, or the same sound, are placed together to create an appealing, catchy sound.

Here are some more examples of alliteration in use:

fleeting fly
mischievous mouse
jumping giants

Alliteration is often used in the names of shops, book titles and newspaper headlines:

Charlie's Chip Shop

The Pirate's Picturebook

GOVERNMENT'S GREAT GAMBLE

Exercise 6.6

Can you think of some appropriate words to put alongside these nouns? Remember to choose words that begin with the same letter each time.

e.g. *sand — soft sand*   *beetle — brave beetle*

1. tiger

2. helicopter

3. sealion

4. fire

5. mountain

6. castle

7. shore

8. kangaroo

You can put more than one adjective before a noun. For example:

big, brave beetle
soft, silky sand

In these examples a **comma** (**,**) is used to separate the first and second adjective.

Exercise 6.7 🖍️

Can you think of **two** adjectives to place before these nouns? Remember you must use words with the same first letters (or the same sound) to make alliteration. Place a comma between your adjectives.

e.g. *greedy, green grasshopper*

1. giant

2. food

3. beach

4. pig

5. hamster

- -

Can you spell?

Making plurals

The word **plural** means more than one in number. To turn most nouns into plurals you just add an –s. For example:

one beetle	*two beetle**s***
one spider	*two spider**s***

But there are some exceptions to this rule. *Fly*, for example, becomes *fl**ies*** when you make it plural. Here are some rules worth remembering.

- If a word ends in **–y** with a consonant in front (a non-vowel letter), then knock off the **–y** and add **–ies**:

baby – babies	*party – parties*

- If a word ends in **–y** with a vowel in front, then just add **–s**:

Toy – toys	*monkey – monkeys*

- If a word ends in **–f**, then knock off the **–f** and add **–ves**:

Leaf – leaves	*wife – wives*

  (but there are exceptions: e.g. *roofs, chiefs*)

- If a word ends in **–o** then add **–es**:

  Potato – potatoes   *hero – heroes*

  (but there are exceptions: e.g. *pianos, studios*)

- If a word ends in a soft sound like **–ch**, **–s**, **–sh** or **–x** then add **–es**:

  Beach – beaches   *marsh – marshes*

Exercise 6.8

Copy these words into your book. Then write the plural for each one. Remember the rules.

1. fox
2. snake
3. map
4. match
5. loaf
6. journey
7. tomato

Exercise 6.9

Identify the singular word from which these plurals are made.

e.g. *watches – watch*

1. charts
2. countries
3. lunches
4. cakes
5. valleys
6. fleas
7. princesses

Speaking and listening

1. How do you react when you see a spider or a wasp? Do you stay calm or do you jump about? Working with a partner, pretend you have just seen an insect that frightens one of you. The other person remains calm and cannot understand what all the fuss is about. Perform your scene for the class.

2. Work in pairs. One of you makes the sound of a bumble bee, while the other one pretends that he or she is just sitting quietly in the garden when the bee arrives. How will the sitter react? Make the sound effects while the other person acts.

3. Choose an insect and put together a class talk about it. Try to use pictures, words and even sound effects if you can. Think about where and when the insect can be found.

4. Play a memory game in a circle. Each person says the following line out loud: *I was hiding in the shed when onto my head fell a… spider.* Each person adds a new insect or other type of creature to the sentence, after repeating what the others have said.

Have you read?

Here are some stories and information books about mini-beasts:

Charlotte's Web by E. B. White (Puffin Books)
James and the Giant Peach by Roald Dahl (Puffin Books)
The Very Busy Spider by Eric Carle (Hamish Hamilton Ltd)
1001 Bugs to Spot by G. Doherty (Usborne Publishing)
Bugs and Minibeasts by John Farndon, Jen Green & Barbara Taylor (Southwater)
Ugly Bugs and Nasty Nature (Horrible Science) by Nick Arnold (Scholastic)
Ladybirds (Minibeasts) by Claire Llewellyn (Franklin Watts Ltd)
Minibeasts (Foundations) by Rachel Sparks-Linfield (A & C Black)

Other things to do...

- Write a story in which the world is attacked by giant insects. What kind of insects might they be? What will happen to the main character(s)? How will the world be saved?

- Work with a friend to put together a 'creepy-crawlies quiz'. Write some questions about different types of insects. Then test your classmates.

- The poem by Leonard Clark is called 'Good Company'. What type of animal would be good company for you, and why? Would it be a dog, or a cat, perhaps? Or something more unusual? Write down your thoughts.

Chapter 7

Greedy Gloop

Poor Augustus Gloop. He never could resist food, and the river of melted chocolate that runs through Mr Wonka's chocolate factory is just too tempting…

Mrs Gloop: Augustus! Augustus, sweetheart! I don't think you had better do that.

Willy Wonka: Oh, no! Please, Augustus, p-l-e-a-s-e! I beg of you not to do that. My chocolate must be untouched by human hands!

5 **Mrs Gloop:** Augustus! Didn't you hear what the man said? Come away from that river at once!

Augustus Gloop: [*Leaning over further*] This stuff is *teee-rrific*! Oh boy, I need a bucket to drink it properly!

Willy Wonka: Augustus… you *must* come away! *You are dirtying my*
10 *chocolate*!

Mrs Gloop: Augustus! You'll be giving that nasty cold of yours to about a million people all over the country! Be careful Augustus! You're leaning *too far out*!!

[Augustus *shrieks as he falls in*]

15 **Mrs Gloop:** Save him! He'll drown! He can't swim a yard! Save him! Save him!

Augustus Gloop: Help! Help! Fish me out!

Mrs Gloop [*To everybody*] Don't just stand there! *Do* something!

Veruca Salt: Look! He's being sucked closer to one of the pipes!

20 **Mike Teavee:** There he goes!

Mrs Gloop: Oh, help! Murder! Police! Augustus! Come back at once! Where are you going? [*Pause*] He's disappeared. He's *disappeared*! Where does that pipe go to? Quick! Call the fire brigade!

Willy Wonka: Keep calm. He'll come out of it just fine, you wait and see.

25 **Mrs Gloop:** But he'll be turned into marshmallows!

Willy Wonka: Impossible!

Mrs Gloop: And why *not*, may I ask?

Willy Wonka: Because that pipe doesn't go anywhere near the Marshmallow Room. It leads to the room where I make a most delicious
30 kind of strawberry-flavoured chocolate-coated fudge.

Mrs Gloop: Oh, my poor Augustus! They'll be selling him by the pound all over the country tomorrow morning! [Willy Wonka *is laughing and* Mrs Gloop *begins to chase him, trying to hit him with her purse.*] How *dare* you laugh like that when my boy's just gone up the pipe! You monster!
35 You think it's a joke, do you? You think that sucking my boy up into your Fudge Room like that is just one great colossal joke?

Willy Wonka: He'll be perfectly safe.

Mrs Gloop: He'll be chocolate fudge!

Willy Wonka: Never! I wouldn't allow it!

40 **Mrs Gloop:** And why not?

Willy Wonka: Because the taste would be *terrible*! Just imagine it! Augustus-flavoured chocolate-coated Gloop! No one would buy it.

Mrs Gloop: I don't want to *think* about it!

Willy Wonka: Nor do I, and I do promise you, madam, that your
45 darling boy *is* perfectly safe.

Mrs Gloop: If he's safe, then where is he? Lead me to him this instant!

Willy Wonka: Go over to one of the Oompa-Loompas and ask him to show you to the Fudge Room. When you get there, take a long stick and start poking around inside the big chocolate-mixing barrel. He should be
50 there. Don't leave him in there too long though, or he's liable to get poured out into the fudge boiler, and that really would be a disaster, wouldn't it? My fudge would become *quite* uneatable!

Mrs Gloop: [*Shrieking*] What … what … *what* did you say?

Willy Wonka: I'm joking – forgive me. Good-bye, Mrs Gloop … see
55 you later.

[Mrs Gloop *exits. All others exit in opposite direction*]

Oompa-Loompas: Augustus Gloop! Augustus Gloop!
The great big greedy nincompoop!
How long could we allow this beast
60 To gorge and guzzle, feed and feast
On everything he wanted to?
Great Scott! It simply wouldn't do!
So what we do in cases such
As this, we use the gentle touch,
65 'Come on!' we cried. 'The time is ripe
To send him shooting up the pipe!'
But don't, dear children, be alarmed;
Augustus Gloop will not be harmed,
Although, of course, we must admit

70	He will be altered quite a bit.
	He'll be quite changed from what he's been,
	When he goes through the fudge machine:
	Slowly, the wheels go round and round,
	The cogs begin to grind and pound;
75	A hundred knives go slice, slice, slice;
	We add some sugar, cream, and spice;
	Then out he comes! And now! By grace!
	This boy, who only just before
	Was loathed by men from shore to shore,
80	This greedy brute, this louse's ear,
	Is loved by people everywhere!
	For who could hate or bear a grudge
	Against a luscious bit of fudge?

(From Roald Dahl's Charlie and the Chocolate Factory — A Play, adapted by Richard George, 1976)

Exercise 7.1 🖊

Read *Greedy Gloop*. Then answer these questions in complete sentences.

1. (a) At the beginning of the passage, why is Augustus Gloop's mother worried?

(b) Why is Willy Wonka worried?

2. Why should it be worrying that Augustus Gloop has a cold? What might happen?

3. Which line in the play tells you that Augustus has actually fallen into the river?

4. What is the first thing Augustus says as he falls in?

5. Suddenly Augustus disappears from view. Where has he gone?

6. What, according to the Oompa-Loompas, will happen to Augustus Gloop?

7. Using a dictionary, write meanings for the following words: (a) *shrieks* (line 14); (b) *delicious* (line 29); (c) *colossal* (line 36); (d) *gorge* (line 60).

Chocolate fudge cake

Do you like chocolate? Ask a grown-up to help you make this delicious recipe for rich chocolate cake topped with a chocolate fudge icing. But don't let him or her eat it all!

Recipe information
Serves: 15
Preparation time: 30 minutes
Cooking time: 50 minutes

5 **Ingredients**
For the cake:
125g plain chocolate
300ml milk
125g brown sugar
10 125g butter or margarine
125g caster sugar
2 medium size eggs, separated
250g plain flour
1 teaspoon bicarbonate of soda

15 **Chocolate fudge icing:**
25g butter or margarine
1-2 tablespoons of milk
125g icing sugar
1 tablespoon of cocoa powder

20 **Recipe**

1. Line and grease a square or rectangular 18 x 28cm baking tin, allowing the paper to come 2.5cm above two opposite sides.

2. Preheat the oven to 180C, 350F, gas mark 4.

3. Place the chocolate, 4 tablespoons of the milk and the brown sugar in 25 a pan and heat gently, stirring until melted. Stir in the remaining milk.

4. Cream the fat and the caster sugar until light and fluffy. Then beat in the egg yolks thoroughly.

5. Sift the flour and the bicarbonate of soda together.

6. Add the creamed mixture with the chocolate mixture and beat until smooth.

30

7. Whisk the egg whites until soft peaks form. Fold a teaspoon into the mixture to lighten it, then carefully fold in the rest.

8. Turn into the prepared tin and bake in the oven for 50 minutes, until the cake springs back when lightly pressed. Turn onto a wire rack to cool slightly.

35

9. To make the icing, place the fat and a tablespoon of milk in a small pan and heat gently until melted. Sift the icing sugar and cocoa together and add to the pan, mixing well and smooth; add a little more milk if necessary.

40

10. Pour over the warm cake and spread evenly to the edges. Allow to set completely, then cut into squares.

(From www.sainsburys.co.uk)

Exercise 7.2

Read the recipe for chocolate fudge cake. Then answer these questions in proper sentences.

1. How long does the fudge cake take to produce, in total?

2. How much butter or margarine do you need for the whole recipe?

3. What should you mix with bicarbonate of soda?

4. How do you know when the cake mixture is cooked?

5. In Chapter 4 you learned about imperative verbs. Write down two imperatives from this recipe.

6. Use a dictionary to find out the meanings of these words: (a) *recipe* (line 20); (b) *grease* (line 21); (c) *preheat* (line 23); (d) *sift* (line 28).

Exercise 7.3

Your turn to write:

1. How do you think Mrs Gloop must feel, seeing her beloved son tumbling into the chocolate river? Write a conversation that she might have with her husband, when she returns home that night.

2. Then write a letter of complaint, from Mr Gloop to Willy Wonka, demanding to know where his son has gone, and what will happen to him.

3. Imagine you are working for Mr Willy Wonka, at his famous chocolate factory. Your job is to attract more visitors everyday. Design a poster that advertises the factory as a 'great day out for all the family'. You might even offer them free chocolate if they come along! Think about: opening times, what they will see, free gifts and how to get there.

4. Is there a particular recipe that you know well? Have you made something delicious at home, with an adult? If you have, then write a recipe for this dish. Remember to use lots of imperative verbs (e.g. *whisk, pour, mix*). If you have not done much cooking at home, then why not invent a wonderful new recipe for an exciting new cake? Think of some unusual ingredients.

Learning about language

Commas in lists

Here are some of the ingredients that you need to make chocolate fudge cake:

You will need milk, sugar, butter, eggs and flour.

Here are some of the tasks you will need to carry out in order to make it:

To make the cake you will need to stir, sift, whisk, mix and cook.

These sentences have something in common. Each includes a **list**. Between each item in the list is a **comma** (**,**). Look again at the sentences and notice how the comma is used to separate the different items into a list, so that readers are not confused.

Here is a third example:

Willy Wonka invited Charlie, Augustus, Veruca, Mike and Violet to his chocolate factory.

Commas in this sentence separate each name in the list of children who visited Mr Wonka's factory.

Commas are used in lists until you get to the final two items, which are then separated by the word **and**:

*…cabbages, carrots, potatoes **and** broccoli.*

*…Mark, Lucy, Ramankur **and** Jason.*

The word **and** brings the list to a neat end. It tells readers that the last item is coming.

Exercise 7.4

Rewrite these sentences putting commas in the correct places.

1. For this recipe I need garlic tomatoes onions and peppers.

2. Will Julie David Greta and Paul please see me at breaktime.

3. During our holiday we went surfing fishing riding and sailing.

4. Our concert tour takes in Manchester Birmingham Bristol Cardiff and London.

5. I can play the clarinet trumpet piano and saxophone.

Exercise 7.5

Now rewrite these sentences, placing commas and the word *and* in the correct places.

1. To make the model you will need pencils glue paper scissors.

2. The Headmaster would like to see Smith Harrison Jenkins Patel Thorpe at lunchtime.

3. In the Autumn term the school offers soccer rugby netball hockey basketball.

4. 'This train will be calling at Reading Swindon Bath Bristol.'

5. I have invited Jake Emma Jemima Lydia Darren to my party on Saturday.

6. On holiday we rode swam walked ate.

7. Our large brown friendly dog came too.

Making contractions

Look at the following sentences from *Greedy Gloop*:

He'll *be chocolate fudge!*

*Never! I **wouldn't** allow it!*

*I **don't** want to think about it!*

The underlined words contain **contractions**. These are two words (or more) that have been **contracted** (or squeezed together) to make one word, by missing out one or more letters.

In the first example, **he'll** was once **he will**. The letters 'w' and 'i' were squeezed out and the remaining letters have been pushed together to make a new word **he'll**. Similarly, **wouldn't** was once **would not** and **don't** was once **do not**.

Here are some more contractions, with their full versions:

I've — I have   *she'd — she had*   *they're — they are*

Can you spot which letters have been missed out?

Contractions are usually found in story speech or play scripts. They are not usually used in more formal writing, like essays or comprehension answers.

• •

Exercise 7.6

Write out these contractions and put their full versions next to them.

1. we're

2. you'll

3. I'd

4. they've

5. I can't

6. we wouldn't

Exercise 7.7

Write out these phrases. Put the contracted version next to each one.

1. I should not

2. you will not

3. you have

4. we are not

5. she will

6. he had

Can you spell?

–le endings

There are many words that end with the letter pattern **–le**. Here are some examples:

fable   *single*   *trundle*

In the words above, the **–le** word-ending (also known as a 'suffix') comes after a **consonant** (*non-vowel letter, e.g. b, g, d*) and this produces a particular sound:

table for example, sounds like *'tay-bull'*

and *jingle* sounds more like *'jin-gull'*.

This **–ull** sound changes to a different sound when the letter pattern **–le** comes after a vowel, e.g.

smile, tile, pale

Provided it follows a consonant, the suffix **–le** always sounds like **–ull** in **gull**, even though it is spelt differently.

Exercise 7.8

Think of a sentence for each of these –le words.

1. crumble

2. middle

3. dangle

4. circle

5. handle

6. angle

Exercise 7.9

Can you guess which –le words are being talked about here? Read the clues and write down the correct words.

1. t - - - le (tied up in a knot)

2. s - - - le (only one)

3. m - - - le (to interfere)

4. s - - - - le (to trip)

5. c - - - le (useful in the dark)

6. r - - - - - - le (four-sided shape)

Speaking and listening

1. With a group of friends, try rehearsing and then performing the scene from *Charlie and the Chocolate Factory*. Decide on your parts. Try to learn the words by heart. Remember to use lots of expression.

2. Working with a partner, perform the conversation which you have written between Mr and Mrs Gloop, as they discuss what has happened to their precious, greedy son.

3. Can you imagine feasting on a giant chocolate bar? How would you feel? Close your eyes and imagine chomping on chocolate. Then describe this feeling, using as many interesting adjectives as you can. If you don't like chocolate, then your description will be very different.

4. Write an acrostic poem about chocolate. Write CHOCOLATE down the side of the page and then use the letters to begin each line. Think about the taste, touch and smell of chocolate. Think about how fat you might become if you eat too much. Remember what happened to Augustus Gloop!

Have you read?

Several of Roald Dahl's classic stories have been made into enjoyable plays. Here are a few of them for you to enjoy reading with your family and friends:

The Twits: Play by David Wood (Samuel French Ltd.)
James and the Giant Peach: A Play by Richard George (Puffin Books)
Fantastic Mr Fox: A Play by Sally Reid (Puffin Books)
The Witches: Play (Acting Edition) by David Wood (Samuel French Ltd.)
Charlie and the Great Glass Elevator: A Play by Richard R. George (Collins)

Here are some collections of Roald Dahl's poems for you to enjoy reading aloud:

Roald Dahl's Revolting Rhymes by Roald Dahl (Puffin Books)
Dirty Beasts by Roald Dahl (Puffin Books)
Rhyme Stew by Roald Dahl (Puffin Books)

Other things to do...

- Read the play script once again. Then extend it, by adding another scene of your own. What might happen next? (You may know the real story.)

- Just how is real chocolate made? Research this lovely subject by checking out books and Internet sites. Put together some information about chocolate and then share it in class. (You never know, your teacher might even allow you to try some too.)

- Practise following a real recipe at home, with an adult. Bring in the recipe after you have used it and describe to the class how you got on. You may even be able to bring in what you have made.

Chapter 8

Dog rescue

When the River Thames freezes over, it can be very dangerous –
even for a dog.

She was the colour and size of a haystack with a brain the size of a
needle. Why else would she have ventured out on to the ice when the
river was thawing? Now she just stood, looking up at the houses on the
bridge, and barking in a slow, tuneless rhythm, like an old man coughing.

5 The ice was slippery. Her paws kept splaying outwards until the cold of
the ice on her belly made her tiptoe back up to her full height. And still
she barked. Someone on the bridge threw a lump of coal at her. It skidded
across the whiteness, leaving a black tail, then plopped into a fissure: the
ice was breaking up.

10 After yet another winter of breathtaking cold, the Thames was finally
remembering its true nature. Growling like something much bigger than a
dog, its ice buckled and broke. Soon the big animal was standing
marooned on a diamond of slippery, rocking ice.

'We have to help her,' said Clay. 'The poor beast will drown!'

15 'It got out there. It can get back,' said Hal doubtfully, but already he was
tapping his foot on the ice, testing whether it would take his weight. The
dog in the middle of the river was far too beautiful to abandon.

The muddy foreshore crackled under their feet like eggshell, then they
were out on the frozen river, calling, all the time calling to the big dog.

20 She turned and looked at the two brothers with sad, despairing eyes, as
if to say, '*I would like to come, but my place is here…*' Then she went back
to barking.

Slipping and teetering, jumping and skidding, Clay and Hal crossed cracks
and gaps in the ice, which at once widened into canyons. Here and there,

25 they glimpsed water, brown and shineless, sliding by beneath them like the
scales of a snake.

'Father will kill us if we get drowned,' said Clay, and his steamy breath
settled on his lashes like tears.

30 Crawling at last on hands and knees, resting their hands on their coat cuffs, Clay and Hal reached the ice island where the dog stood bark-bark-barking.

Close to, she looked as big as a horse. When Hal stepped on to her raft of ice, she turned round twice then stood up on her hind paws, the front two on his shoulders, her nose against his. The look in her eyes was 35 pleading. In fact it was almost as sorrowful as their situation.

Icy water washed over their feet. The ice fragment rocked wildly. The crazy paving of the river began to move, the pieces jostling each other for elbow-room. The dog began to lunge to and fro, making things worse. It was like trying to stand teetering on a wet toboggan as it sets off 40 downhill.

'I don't like it here,' said Clay (who was, after all, only seven).

(From Dog Days by Geraldine McCaughrean, 2003)

Exercise 8.1 ✏️

Read the passage from *Dog Days* and then answer the following questions in complete sentences.

1. Write a word from the first passage that tells you that the author is talking about a dog.

2. Why was it dangerous to be out on the icy river at this time?

3. Where did the lump of coal come from?

4. What sort of noise did the ice make, as it broke up?

5. How did Clay and Hal manage to keep their hands warm as they crawled across the ice?

6. Write meanings for the following words. You may use a dictionary to help you. (a) *ventured* (line 2); (b) *fissure* (line 9); (c) *marooned* (line 13); (d) *sorrowful* (line 35).

Whale meets his Jonah

A seven tonne northern bottle-nosed whale was spotted by a sleepy commuter at 8.30am today, causing him to wonder if had missed his connection. However, the animal was indeed struggling in the murky waters of the Thames, close to the Houses of Parliament. It may not have
5 had plans for the overthrow of government but it is causing a great stir amongst the London crowds and rescue workers.

The 5m whale is not usually seen in British waters; bottle-nosed whales are normally found in the deep seas of the North Atlantic. Experts are baffled as to why it has made its way up the Thames, but it may have
10 become disorientated. Previously it had been seen east of the Thames Barrier with two other whales who have now disappeared.

Vets and other experts from the British Divers Marine Life Rescue and the RNLI are on hand to offer any assistance and to prevent the whale from beaching. It has already injured itself by crashing into an empty
15 boat. The workers' main concern is the animal's welfare but, once disorientated, whales are often difficult customers to assist. It is feared

that if all efforts to re-direct the whale back to the open seas fail, they may have to put it down to prevent its further suffering.

Alison Shaw, a manager of the Marine and Freshwater Conservation
20 Programme at the Zoological Society of London said, 'It is a relatively mature animal, a long way from home. We have no idea why it is here but the fact that it is swimming upstream is not a good sign. The whale must be confused or ill.'

(20th January 2006)

Exercise 8.2

Read the passage entitled *Whale meets his Jonah* and then answer these questions in proper sentences.

1. (a) How heavy is the whale?

    (b) What is its length?

2. Where would you normally expect to find a bottle-nosed whale?

3. How did the whale injure itself?

4. The writer suggests that whales are difficult animals to help, once they become lost. Why do you think this is true?

5. Why do you think Alison Shaw is so concerned about the whale swimming upstream?

6. Write down two words from the final paragraph that tell you the whale is quite old.

7. Write dictionary definitions for the following words: (a) *commuter* (line 2); (b) *murky* (line 3); (c) *baffled* (line 9); (d) *disorientated* (line 10).

Exercise 8.3

Your turn to write:

1. Imagine that you are Hal or Clay from the passage above. Rewrite the first few paragraphs of this passage as a **first person narrative**. Include your own thoughts about what you think will happen to the dog and to you. Will everything be all right?

2. Read the passage from *Dog Days* once again. Then continue the story in your own words. What do you think happens next? Will the dog be rescued? What do you think will happen to Hal and Clay when they arrive home, cold and wet?

3. Write a story about the whale that was spotted in the River Thames. Where is he or she going? And why? How will the story end? Use your imagination – in stories, anything is possible. Don't forget to give the whale a name.

4. Imagine that a different animal from the wild appears in a different place in a big city – like a market, a museum or a shopping centre. What type of animal will it be? What will happen to it? Write your own news report – just like the one in the passage – describing when and where the animal was spotted.

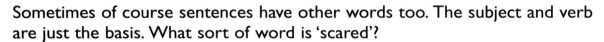

Learning about language

Subjects and verbs

In Chapter 3 you will have learned the rule that most sentences need a **subject** and every sentence needs a **verb**. For example:

The   ice   cracked.
subject   *verb*

 Clay   felt   scared.
subject *verb*

Sometimes of course sentences have other words too. The subject and verb are just the basis. What sort of word is 'scared'?

Another important rule to remember is that the subject in a sentence must **agree** with the verb. The word 'agree' means match up. For example, you will notice that there is something wrong with these sentences:

The children was frightened.

They tries to rescue the dog.

The verb and the subject do not match up. The sentences should read:

*The children **were** frightened.*

*They **try** to rescue the dog.*

Always make sure that the verb matches up with the subject, whether it is in the first, second or third person, singular or plural:

	Singular		Plural	
First person	I	was/try	we	were/try
Second person	you	were/try	you	were/try
Third person	he, she, it	was/tries	they	were/try

Exercise 8.4

Copy out these sentences, choosing the correct verb from the brackets. Always make sure the subject and the verb agree.

1. The ice ———— to crack and break up. (begin / begins)

2. Clay says 'We ———— to help rescue the dog.' (has / have)

3. Hal and Clay ———— across the ice. (crawls / crawl)

4. The crowds ———— the whale in the Thames. (watch / watches)

5. The whale ———— a long way from home. (is / are)

Exercise 8.5

Can you spot the mistakes in these sentences? Rewrite each one, making sure that the subject and the verb agree.

1. The dog were unhappy.

2. The children feels scared on the ice.

3. The whale are a long way from home.

4. Vets is remaining on standby.

5. The rescuers says it is the first whale they has seen in the Thames.

Conjunctions

Conjunctions are very useful words. They are joining words. They can join small sentences to make one bigger sentence. Look at this example:

The ice was thawing. The dog was in danger.

*The ice was thawing **and** the dog was in danger.*

One small word like **and** can help you to connect sentences together, and make your writing sound much better. Too many short sentences, like those in the first example, can sound jerky, although all good writing has sentences in a variety of shapes, including short and long.

Three conjunctions you will often see are: **and**, **or** and **but**. For example:

The whale swam upstream. It was spotted by a man on a train.

+ and

*The whale swam upstream **and** was spotted by a man on a train.*

Should we pull the whale out now? Should we wait to see if it swims downstream?

+ or

*Should we pull the whale out now **or** should we wait to see if it swims downstream?*

The dog tried to run back to the river bank. The ice beneath it cracked and shifted.

+ but

*The dog tried to run back to the river bank **but** the ice beneath it cracked and shifted.*

· ·

Exercise 8.6

Copy these sentences and fill in the gaps with *and*, *or* or *but*.

1. On Saturday we went horse riding ———— then we went swimming.

2. Jeremy wanted to join us ———— he could not come.

3. Are you comfortable ———— would you like an extra pillow?

4. I like dogs ———— I prefer cats.

5. The winning team marched off the field _____ the crowd cheered as they left.

6. We could cook a meal at home _____ we could visit a restaurant tonight.

Exercise 8.7

Use **and**, **or** or **but** to join these sentences. Look at the examples above if you need help. Don't forget you will need to adjust the punctuation – capital letters and sentence endings.

1. Would you like some more apple pie? Have you enough?

2. Sophia wanted to play outside. It was pouring with rain.

3. We spent two weeks in Australia. Then we flew to New Zealand.

4. Mikey washed the dishes. His mother dried them.

5. I tried to get a table in your favourite restaurant. It was fully booked.

6. Will you come here? Shall I come round to you?

Can you spell?
Words with qu–

The letter pattern **qu–** should be quite familiar to you. There are lots of words that begin with these letters, for example:

queen   quiet   quick

When **qu–** is used to begin a word, the sound created is more like a **qw**. But the letter –'u' always comes after the 'q'.

There are other words that have **–qu–** in the middle of them:

conquer   technique

Here the sound of the letters has changed from 'qw' to **k**. But the letter pattern is still the same.

You will never see an English word that contains a 'q' without a 'u' next to it. So you might as well get used to writing these two letters together.

Remember: wherever there is a **q**, you need a **u**.

Exercise 8.8

How many words with *–qu* can you spot in this *quick* wordsearch? There are ten in total. Write a word down in your book every time you find one.

c	q	u	a	r	t	e	r	z	q
b	g	t	n	x	e	g	w	u	l
a	c	h	e	q	u	e	e	l	h
l	o	q	a	q	y	s	f	i	e
w	n	r	u	u	t	g	v	q	i
p	q	u	p	i	n	w	m	u	k
w	u	e	o	t	e	f	e	o	c
x	e	n	y	e	d	t	t	r	i
c	r	o	i	t	w	c	y	u	u
z	k	c	a	u	q	l	x	v	q

Exercise 8.9

Write six sentences to show the meanings of these *qu–* words. You may need to use a dictionary to help you.

1. banquet
2. question
3. liquor

4. quiet
5. quality
6. technique

Speaking and listening

1. How do you think the man might have felt when he first saw a whale in the river Thames? Working with a partner, imagine you are two workers going to work in London on the train. One of you spots the whale in the River Thames, but the other person misses it. The person who saw it must convince the other that (s)he *really did* see a whale.

2. In pairs, play a game of word tennis, in which you take turns to call out different words that begin with the letter pattern *wh–*. When someone hesitates or repeats a word, then the other player wins a point. Write the words down at the end, and see how many you have thought of.

3. Hold a discussion about favourite animals. Give reasons to explain why you like the animals you do. Is there a most popular animal in the class? Is it the whale, perhaps?

4. Play a memory game, in which you take turns to say the following line:

   Hey! Guess what I saw in the Thames today… a _____ !

   You must fill in the gap with an exciting animal or object, but first you must remember what everyone else has said and list them in order.

Have you read?

Here are some stories and information books about rivers and seas:

Journey to the River Sea by Eva Ibbotson (Longman)
A Gift from Winklesea by Helen Cresswell (Hodder Children's Books)
Little Tim and the Brave Sea Captain by Edward Ardizzone (Frances Lincoln Children's Books)
Horrible Harry Goes to Sea by Suzy Kline (Puffin Books)
The Kingdom under the Sea by Joan Aiken (Puffin Books)
Little Turtle and the Song of the Sea by Sheridan Cain (Little Tiger Press)
Raging Rivers (Horrible Geography) by Anita Ganeri (Scholastic Hippo)
I Wonder Why the Sea is Salty by Anita Ganeri (Kingfisher Ltd)
Rivers by Nicola Edwards (Hodder Wayland)
Investigating Rivers by Clare Hibbert (Evans Brothers Ltd)

Other things to do...

- Find out more about the River Thames. Where does it begin and where does it flow to? You could use atlases, encyclopaedias and Internet sites to find your information. Then share what you have found out in class.

- Have you ever seen a frozen river, like the one in *Dog Days*? What was it like? Describe a place you have visited that looked beautiful in the snow or ice. It could be a river, a lake, a pond, or some other natural place, like a mountain range. Use lots of interesting and strange nouns and verbs to bring your writing to life.

- Do you have a pet dog? Perhaps you have a cat, or a hamster? Write a description of your pet – or a pet you would like to have. Think about why it is precious to you, like Hal and Clay's dog in the passage above.

Chapter 9

Silvery Moon

I dreamed of monsters late last night
And woke to find my room was light;
Not sunshine bright as in the day,
But gently shining where I lay.

5 To my window then I crept,
While the household quietly slept.
I softly drew the curtains wide
And stood up tall to peek outside.

A vision in a window frame!
10 Familiar – and yet not the same.
The lawn spread smoothly down below
And shimmered in a glimm'ring glow.

Beneath the oak tree's friendly shade,
Silvery shadows ran and played;
15 The holly bush stood, sparkly, stark,
Prickly glittering, light and dark.

This homely plot I know so well,
Now captured in this magic spell;
This special change in all I see;
20 What can this mean, how can this be?

And in my questing, wondering why?
I raise my eyes up to the sky,
Where rides the moon, its friendly face
Smiling down through boundless space.

25 Why, there's the answer – Man's Old Friend,
Whose silken rays our troubles mend.
His kindly presence fills my head.
Monsters banished – back to bed!

(by Alan Hammond, 2007)

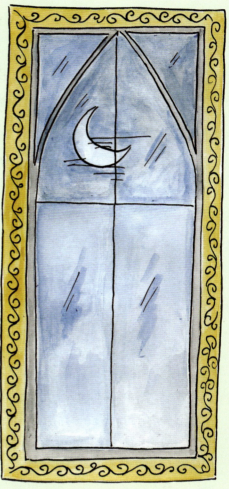

Exercise 9.1 ✏

Read the poem 'Silvery Moon'. Then answer the following questions in complete sentences.

1. What was unusual about the speaker's room when he woke up in the middle of the night?

2. Where did he go after he got out of bed?

3. Write down a line from the poem which tells you the speaker is all alone.

4. Why did the garden look so different?

5. In what way does the last verse of the poem reminds us of the first verse? What do they have in common?

6. Can you spot a rhyming pattern in this poem? Describe it in your own words.

7. Use a dictionary to help you write meanings for the following words:
   (a) *household* (line 6); (b) *peek* (line 8); (c) *homely* (line 17);
   (d) *banished* (line 28).

A giant leap for mankind

On 20th July, 1969, Neil Armstrong clambered down the ladder of the lunar module Eagle and became the first human being to stand on the surface of the Moon. The History News gave a glowing report of this monumental milestone in the history of space exploration…

5 One-fifth of the entire population of the world watched TV in wonder as American astronaut Neil Armstrong stepped on to the surface of the Moon.

'That's one small step for a man, one giant leap for mankind,' his voice echoed round mission control at Houston, Texas, 384 000 kilometres away.

10 A few seconds later, Armstrong was joined on the surface by Edwin 'Buzz' Aldrin. The third member of the crew, Michael Collins, was still in orbit around the Moon. He had remained in *Apollo 11's* command module *Columbia*.

The three men left Earth in their space capsule *Apollo 11* on 16th July,
15 thrust into space by its awesomely powerful *Saturn 5* rocket.

It was around noon four days later when Armstrong and Aldrin first
crawled into the *Apollo* lunar module – the *Eagle* – to begin the descent
procedure. Half an hour later, Collins pressed the button that released
the *Eagle* from *Columbia* and sent it on its way down to the Moon.
20 Minutes later, Armstrong told mission control, 'The *Eagle* has landed.' The
answer from mission control was a huge sigh of relief, and a message
went back to the Moon saying, 'We're breathing again. Thanks a lot.'

Armstong's next task was to pull a cord on the *Eagle* and lower a live
television camera. A few minutes later, 600 million people watched him
25 take his historic steps.

(From The History News: In Space by Michael Johnstone, 1999)

Exercise 9.2

Read *A giant leap for mankind* and then answer these questions in proper sentences.

1. What nationality was Neil Armstrong?

2. What was the name of the astronauts' space capsule?

3. How long did it take Armstrong and his crew to reach the moon?

4. (a) What was the first thing Neil Armstrong said to mission control when his lunar module landed on the Moon?

   (b) How did the people in mission control react to this news?

5. How were the people on Earth able to watch Armstrong's first steps on the Moon?

6. Write down dictionary definitions for the following words: (a) *milestone* (line 4); (b) *mission* (line 9); (c) *descent* (line 17); (d) *historic* (line 25).

Exercise 9.3

Your turn to write:

1. Write your own poem about the Moon. You can write about the effect that the Moon has on Earth, as the poet has done in 'Silvery Moon', or you may choose to imagine you are standing on the Moon. What does it look like? What can you see?

2. Write your own newspaper report describing the scenes on Earth when *Apollo 11* returns to Earth and the brave astronauts are welcomed home. Include pictures, eyewitness accounts, opinions and descriptions of the scene.

3. Write a short story about the first mission to Mars. Do the astronauts make it that far? Will they be able to land on Mars? What will it be like? How will the people on Earth react? Try to make your story as exciting as possible.

4. Imagine you are Neil Armstrong. Write down your account of the lunar landing in a pretend diary or captain's log. Remember to include not only what you saw and heard, but how you felt also, as you took those historic first steps...

Learning about language

Introducing adverbs

Adverbs usually tell us more about the verbs in a sentence. You might say they **add** to the **verb** (add-verb). Here is an example:

The astronaut stepped bravely onto the Moon.

The word **bravely** is an adverb. It tells us more about **how** the astronaut **stepped** onto the Moon.

Here is another example:

Back on Earth, the crowds watched excitedly.

Here the adverb **excitedly** tells us how the crowds **watched**. It describes how the verb is being performed. Many (but NOT all) adverbs end with the letter pattern **–ly**.

Adverbs help to bring your writing to life. Most adverbs show us **how**, **where** or **when** an action takes place:

*they landed **safely*** (**how**)

*Arstrong stepped **outside*** (**where**)

*Buzz Aldrin joined him **later*** (**when**)

Exercise 9.4

Copy these sentences. Then underline the adverb in each one.

1. The poet crept silently towards the window.

2. Excitedly he gazed up at the silvery Moon.

3. The Moon was shining outside.

4. The crew at Mission Control watched nervously as Armstrong stepped out of the lunar module.

5. Back on Earth, millions of people waited patiently for news of the mission.

6. The families of the astronauts hoped their loved ones would return soon.

Exercise 9.5

Can you think of a sentence for each of these adverbs? Remember that an adverb describes the action, or verb, in a sentence.

1. happily

2. proudly

3. above

4. later

5. slowly

Prepositions

Read the following sentence:

The astronauts landed their lunar module **on** *the moon.*

The word **on** is a preposition. It tells us the **position** of the lunar module. Prepositions tells us the position that one thing has in relation to another. Here are some more examples. The preposition is underlined each time.

The space ship roared <u>across</u> the sky.

It sailed <u>beyond</u> the clouds.

Some words, can act as both prepositions and adverbs. The word **inside** is an example:

The astronauts sat <u>inside</u> the space capsule. (preposition)

The astronauts waited <u>inside</u>. (adverb)

In the first sentence, the word 'inside' is immediately followed by a noun (the space capsule), so it is a **preposition**.

In the second example, it is not followed by anything, so it is an **adverb**.

Prepositions are always placed between two nouns (or pronouns). They include words like:

above, below, beside, near, opposite, over, through and *upon*.

Exercise 9.6

Copy out these sentences. Underline the preposition in each one.

1. They walked beside the river bank.
2. Michael and Janet played on the tennis court.
3. The flowers were placed in a vase.
4. There were lots of presents under the tree.
5. The letters came through the letter-box.
6. I found an old football behind the fence.

Exercise 9.7

Choose the most suitable preposition from the words below to complete each of these sentences:

through   beneath   in   beside   towards   over   near   along

1. I felt ———— the Moon when I won the competition.

2. The children were hiding ———— the table.

3. The train blew its whistle as it passed ———— the tunnel.

4. The aeroplane climbed ———— the sun.

5. Jake walked ———— the path ———— the canal.

6. The tractor was kept ———— the barn ———— the old stable.

Can you spell?

Compound words

Some words that we use are actually made up of two smaller words joined together. These are called **compound words**. Look at these examples:

spaceship – space + ship

moonlight – moon + light

You can see how these words are built up of two separate nouns, both with different meanings. But when they are put together, a new meaning is created. Here are some more compound words you may recognise:

football   matchbox   homework

Exercise 9.8

Join one word from the first box with another from the second box to make a compound word. Write the new words into your book. There are ten possible words.

foot	mark
table	pot
book	ball
goal	path
tooth	brush
tea	cloth
	shelf
	keeper
	paste
	set

Exercise 9.9

Write a sentence for each of these compound words.

1. tracksuit

2. schoolteacher

3. horseriding

4. swimsuit

5. goalpost

6. suitcase

Speaking and listening

1. With a friend, prepare and perform a short interview in which one of you is Neil Armstrong and the other plays the part of a television interviewer. Imagine that this is Armstrong's first interview since his historic mission to the Moon.

2. Working with a friend once again, perform a short role-play in which two astronauts are sharing their thoughts just before their rocket takes off for the Moon. How do they feel? What are they thinking? Will they make it safely back home?

3. Pretend you are a television newsreader. Prepare a short report announcing the successful mission to the Moon. Begin with a really exciting headline. Then give viewers some details about the historic mission. You can find these details in the passage above.

4. In a large circle, take turns to call out an exciting adjective to describe the journey to the Moon. Think about the sights and sounds inside (and outside) the space craft. Then take turns to do the same for the Moon itself. Make your words as interesting as possible.

Have you read?

Here are some stories and information books about the Moon:

Moon Tales by Rina Singh (Bloomsbury)
Moon Maiden by Jean Henry (Flame Tree Publishing Co Ltd)
Papa, Please Get the Moon for Me by Eric Carle (Simon & Schuster)
Goodnight, Moon by Margaret Wise Brown (Campbell Books)
The Moon Dragon by Tony Abbott (Scholastic Paperbacks)
The Man on the Moon by Simon Bartram (Templar Publishing)

Destination Moon & Explorers on the Moon (The Adventures of Tintin)
by Hergé (Egmont)
I Took the Moon for a Walk by Carolyn Curtis (Barefoot Books Ltd)
The First Moon Landing by Gilliam Clements (Franklin Watts)
The Moon Landing by Nigel Kelly (Heinemann)

Other things to do...

- What do you know about the Moon? Use books, magazines and Internet sites to find out more. Put together a short class talk. Use pictures as well as words, to make your talk lively and interesting.

- Would you like to be an astronaut when you are older? Write your thoughts about what you would most like to be when you are grown up. Try to include reasons to explain your choice.

- Do you think there is life on the Moon? Do you think there might be life on Mars? Is it possible that Earth has the only life forms in the universe? Write a few lines to describe the kinds of creatures that might be out there, watching us. Draw some pictures too.

- Make a comic strip of an adventure to the moon. Draw a set of pictures on a sheet of paper and write some sentences beneath each one to show what is happening. Use lots of interesting colours and don't forget to include some aliens, too.

Chapter 10

Worth the wait

Living in Africa, Bertie has developed a great interest in wild animals, and the waterhole he can see from his house proves to be full of surprises…

There was a waterhole downhill from the farmhouse, and some distance away. That waterhole, when there was water in it, became Bertie's whole world. He would spend hours in the dusty compound, his hands gripping the fence, looking out at the wonders of the veld, at the giraffes drinking,
5   spread-legged, at the waterhole; at the browsing impala, tails twitching, alert; at the warthogs snorting and snuffling under the shade of the shingayi trees; at the baboons, the zebras, the wildebeests, and the elephants bathing in the mud. But the moment Bertie always longed for was when a pride of lions came padding out of the veld. The impala were
10 the first to spring away, then the zebra would panic and gallop off. Within seconds the lions would have the waterhole to themselves, and they would crouch to drink.

From the safe haven of the compound Bertie looked and learned as he grew up. By now, he could climb the tree by the farmhouse, and sit high in
15 its banches. He could see better from up there. He would wait for his lions for hours on end. He got to know the life of the waterhole so well that he could feel the lions were out there, even before he saw them.

Bertie had no friends to play with, but he always said he was never lonely as a child. At night he loved reading his books and losing himself in the
20 stories, and by day his heart was out in the veld with the animals. That was where he yearned to be. Whenever his mother was well enough, he would beg her to take him outside the compound, but her answer was always the same.

'I can't, Bertie. Your father has forbidden it,' she'd say. And that was that…

25 …Week in, week out, Bertie had to stay behind his fence. He made up his mind though, that if no-one would take him out into the veld, then one day he would go by himself. But something always held him back. Perhaps it was one of those tales he'd been told of black mamba snakes whose bite would kill you within ten minutes, of hyenas whose jaws would

30　crunch you to bits, of vultures who would finish off anything that was left so that no-one would ever find even the bits. For the time being he stayed behind the fence. But the more he grew up, the more his compound became a prison to him.

One evening – Bertie must have been about six years old by now – he
35　was sitting high up in the branches of his tree, hoping against hope the lions might come down for their sunset drink as they often did. He was thinking of giving up, for it would soon be too dark to see much now, when he saw a solitary lioness come down to the waterhole. Then he saw that she was not alone. Behind her, and on unsteady legs, came what
40　looked like a lion cub – but it was white, glowing white in the gathering gloom of dusk.

While the lioness drank, the cub played at catching her tail; and then, when she had had her fill, the two of them slipped away into the long grass and were gone.

veld = open country or grassland in Africa

(From The Butterfly Lion by Michael Morpurgo, 1996)

Exercise 10.1 ✏️

Read the passage from *The Butterfly Lion*. Then answer these questions in complete sentences.

1. Which animals did Bertie often see under the shade of the shingayi trees?

2. What would make the impala and the zebra flee the waterhole from time to time?

3. Where did Bertie manage to find a better viewpoint from which to see the lions?

4. Describe, in your own words, one of the frightening tales that Bertie had been told about the wild animals in the veld.

5. Why do you think this passage has been entitled *Worth the wait*? What do you think this title is referring to?

6. Write dictionary definitions for the following words: (a) *browsing* (line 5); (b) *haven* (line 13); (c) *yearned* (line 21); (d) *forbidden* (line 24).

• •

Lion family

A pride of lions hunts together, feeds together, and raises its cubs together. Lions are the only cats to live in family groups. Most big cats live alone.

5   **The lionesses** (female lions) do most of the hunting for the pride. They stick together, growling softly to keep in touch.

After the kill, the pride members take it in turns to eat. The males eat first, the females eat second and any cubs eat last. The cubs get such poor scraps that many of them weaken and die.

Female cubs stay in the same pride all their lives, so they are usually all
10 related. Sisters, aunts, nieces and cousins all help with each other's cubs. They will even suckle them if they have milk.

Male lions defend a pride's territory by spraying its borders with urine, roaring loudly at dawn and dusk, and attacking other lions who dare to

appear. Lions have a deafening roar. In the still of the night, they may be
15 heard about 8km away.

How big is a pride of lions?

About 15 animals – one or two males, five or six females and a handful of youngsters and cubs.

What do lions do when they're hot hunting?

20 They spend most of the time sleeping – sometimes as much as 10 hours a day!

Do all lions live in Africa?

No. About 300 lions live in India. They are called Asian lions.

Did you know?

25 • A bushy mane makes a lion look bigger and scares away rival males.

• About 10 000 years ago, there were lions living in Europe.

• Lions (and also tigers) can kill animals larger than themselves.

(From Max Fax: Big Cats by Claire Llewellyn, 2001)

Exercise 10.2

Read the passage entitled *Lion family* and then answer the following questions in complete sentences.

1. Lions live in family groups. Why is this unusual?

2. Why do many lion cubs die young?

3. Write down two ways in which a male lion defends the territory of its pride.

4. Where else might you find lions in the wild, other than in Africa?

5. There may be several similarities between lions and tigers. What is the one mentioned here?

6. Use a dictionary to find out the meanings of the following words:
   (a) *related* (line 10); (b) *territory* (line 12); (c) *borders* (line 12);
   (d) *dusk* (line 13).

Exercise 10.3

Your turn to write:

1. Imagine you are Bertie from *The Butterfly Lion*. Write a description of how it felt finally to see a beautiful lion cub with its mother, down by the waterhole. Describe the scene in the form of a diary, which Bertie might keep.

2. Write a short story of your own about a wild lion cub, growing up in Africa. Describe the kinds of things it might do during the day. Then introduce some danger into your story, which might come from hunters, who are keen to capture lions. Will the lion, and its mother, survive?

3. Look again at the second text, which gives lots of interesting information about lions. Present these fascinating facts in your own information text on lions. Include pictures, diagrams, maps and lots of interesting sentences. You may be able to find more information from the Internet or encyclopaedias.

4. Write a poem all about lions in the wild in Africa. Read the two passages again for ideas. Describe the lion's habitat really carefully, thinking about the sights, sounds and the smells of the African veld.

Learning about language
Verb tenses

As you will have learned from Chapter 3, verbs are **doing words** that tell us the action that is taking place in a sentence. For example:

*Bertie **climbed** a tree.*

The **tense** of the verb tells us when that action takes place – and this can be in the **past**, **present** or **future**. In the example given, the verb **to climb** is written in the past tense. It could also have been written in the present or future tenses:

Present: *Bertie **climbs** a tree (or Bertie **is climbing** a tree)*

Future: *Bertie **will climb** a tree.*

The **present** tense is used when the action is taking place right now:

I walk, I am walking, he walks, he is walking

The **past** tense is used when the action has already taken place. It happened in the past.

I walked, I was walking, I have walked

The **future** tense is used when the action is going to happen in the future:

I shall walk, I am going to walk, I shall be walking

There are many verbs that behave in similar ways, when you change them into a different tense. These are called **regular** verbs. The ways in which we can change regular verbs into the different tenses can be shown in this table for the verb *to look*:

	Present tense	Past tense	Future tense
Singular	I look	I (have) looked	I shall look
	you look	you (have) looked	you will look
	he/she/it looks	he/she/it (has) looked	he/she/it will look
Plural	we look	we (have) looked	we shall look
	you look	you (have) looked	you will look
	they look	they (have) looked	they will look

Simple rules which work for most verbs:

For the **present tense** just knock off the word 'to' and use the main verb name (e.g. to smile – I smile). But add **–s** onto the end if it is **he, she**, or **it**.

For the past tense, add **–ed** onto the end of the main verb name (e.g. I smil**ed**).

For the future tense, use the main verb name and add **shall** or **will** just before it (e.g. I shall smile).

. . . .

Exercise 10.4

Put these regular verbs in the **past** tense.

e.g. *I play – I played*

1. I sail

2. it happens

3. you greet

4. we laugh

5. she uses

6. they watch

7. it rains

8. I kick

9. you wait

10. he listens

· ·

Exercise 10.5

Complete this table of regular verbs. Pay attention to the word that comes before the verb too (e.g. *I, you, he, we, you,* or *they*).

Verb	Present tense	Past tense	Future tense
to sew	I sew		I shall sew
	he washes	he washed	
to listen			you will listen
		they grinned	
	we marched		

As you learn more about verbs, you will begin to realise that there are plenty of others that do not follow these simple rules. These are called **irregular verbs**. Look out for them.

· ·

Double negatives

Common negative words include: **no, not, never, nothing** and **nobody**. Contractions which end in **n't** – which is short for **not** – are also negative words: for example, **can't, didn't** and **won't**.

Here are some negative words in use:

I found nobody in the house.
I have eaten nothing.

If you put two negative words together, they **cancel** one another out.
For example:

I didn't find nobody in the house

…actually means you must have found somebody.

or… *I haven't eaten nothing* actually means you must have eaten something.

So never place a negative word (particularly a negative contraction) before another negative, or you will say the opposite of what you mean.

Exercise 10.6

Copy out these sentences and use the appropriate negative word from the words below to fill in the blanks.

nowhere   never   no-one   not   nothing

1. Mary had ———— been swimming before.

2. I do ———— want any more supper, thank you.

3. We are getting ———— . Let's start again.

4. I know ———— about the crime.

5. ———— has seen the cat since yesterday lunchtime.

Exercise 10.7

These sentences contain double negatives, so they mean the opposite of what they should mean. Rewrite each one in the correct way. You may need to exchange some words for new ones.

1. 'I haven't done nothing wrong!' protested the boy.

2. 'I can't do nothing for you until Tuesday,' said the plumber.

3. 'I didn't have no breakfast this morning,' said Mike, hungrily.

4. 'I won't never do it again,' said Peter.

5. 'There aren't no spaces in the car park,' said Dad.

Can you spell?

Other words for said

The word **said** may be one of the most common words found in stories. It is a very useful verb indeed, because it shows us who said the words that appear in story speech.

For example:

'Look! There's the lion cub!' said Bertie.

'I can't see it!' his mother said.

These sentences are perfectly correct, but the word **said** prevents us from really knowing **how** the characters are speaking. Are they excited? Are they scared, perhaps? We could rewrite these sentences using other verbs instead of *said*:

'Look! There's the lion cub!' cried Bertie.

'I can't see it!' his mother exclaimed.

Now we can imagine Bertie and his mother feeling very **excited**. However, if we use two more words, we can change the scene further:

'Look! There's the lion cub!' whispered Bertie.

'I can't see it!' his mother murmured.

Now it sounds as if the two of them are very close to the lions, because they are having to speak very softly.

The word *said* can be very effective sometimes, and it is certainly worth using. But try, occasionally, to search for something more exciting when you are writing some story speech.

Exercise 10.8

Rewrite these sentences, replacing the word *said* with something more appropriate from the words below:

begged   teased   boasted   enquired   moaned

1. 'Brilliant! I've won the competition for the third time!' said Nigel.

2. 'Excuse me, is the library open this evening?' Miss Jackson said.

3. 'Please can I have some pudding – I'm starving!' said Timothy, greedily.

4. 'But I don't want to go shopping,' Julie said.

5. 'You always lose your glasses, Dad!' said Paulo.

Exercise 10.9

Write down ten other words for said. Then use them in sentences of your own.

e.g. *yelled – 'Goal!' yelled the referee, seconds before half-time.*

Speaking and listening

1. Look again at the first passage. Work with a partner. Prepare a short role-play in which one of you is Bertie and the other is his mother. Bertie has just returned from his lookout post where he saw a real-life lion cub. He's very excited!

2. Put together a short class talk on a particular big cat – you could choose a lion, tiger, cheetah, puma, leopard or black panther. Find interesting information about your chosen big cat, from encyclopaedias, magazines and Internet sites.

3. If you were lucky enough to enjoy a safari holiday in Africa, which animal would you most like to see, and why? Share your thoughts with the class. Perhaps you have already been on a safari holiday and you have some stories to tell...

4. Should lions and other wild animals be kept in zoos and safari parks? Or should they be left in the wild? Can you think of some reasons why we should have zoos? Can you think of some reasons why we should not? Join in a class discussion about whether animals should be kept in zoos and safari parks.

Have you read?

Here are some stories about lions and other jungle animals:

The Jungle Book by Rudyard Kipling (Puffin Books)
Just So Stories by Rudyard Kipling (Walker Books)
The Jungle House by Julia Donaldson (Barrington Stoke Ltd)
Monkey Puzzle by Julia Donaldson (Macmillan Children's Books)
We're Going on a Lion Hunt by David Axtell (Macmillan Children's Books)
Tom's Sausage Lion by Michael Morpurgo (Corgi Children's Books)
The Butterfly Lion by Michael Morpurgo (Collins)
Tiger! by Geoffrey Malone (Hodder Children's Books)
Tigers at Twilight by Mary Pope Osborne (Random House Children's Books)

Other things to do...

- Continue the story of *The Butterfly Lion* in your own words, starting from where the passage finishes. Will Bertie see the lion cub and its mother again? What will happen to them?

- Write your own short story about a big cat – like a lion or tiger – which escapes from a zoo. What will happen? How will he be rescued? Or will he find his way back to the wild, where his old friends are waiting for him!

- Design a poster about your favourite wild animal. Use lots of interesting colours and include a short description – the kind you might see on the cages of a zoo or safari park. Think about its natural home (called a 'habitat'), what it likes to eat, how old it will live to, where it comes from, etc.